A KENTUCKY BOY GOES TO SEA AS A NAVAL OFFICER
Published by Hellgate Press
(An imprint of L&R Publishing, LLC)

Hellgate Press
PO Box 3531
Ashland, OR 97520
email: sales@hellgatepress.com

Cover & Interior Design: L. Redding
ISBN: 978-1-954163-43-0

Printed and bound in the United States of America
First edition 10 9 8 7 6 5 4 3 2 1

This book is dedicated to my colleagues and shipmates in the U.S. Navy who supported me throughout my career and likewise to my colleagues in the Navy of South Vietnam who became like my brothers as did the members of the Armada de Argentina during my tour as an embedded exchange officer in their Navy. I also dedicate this book to the members of the Spanish Navy with whom I worked during my tour as an attaché in Madrid. Finally, I dedicate this book to the Vietnamese refugees I was able to help rescue as Saigon was falling.

A Kentucky Boy
Goes to Sea as
a Naval Officer

A MEMOIR

CDR MARSHALL V.S. HALL, U.S.N. (RET.)

HELLGATE PRESS   ASHLAND, OREGON

A KENTUCKY BOY GOES TO SEA AS A NAVAL OFFICER

Contents

A KENTUCKY BOY GOES TO SEA AS A NAVAL OFFICER

Introduction

My name is Marshall Van Sant Hall. I am a retired U.S. Navy Commander. When I was awarded a full NROTC (Naval Officer Reserve Training Corps) scholarship to Miami University in Oxford, Ohio, in 1968, I became the first person in my family to attend college. At the same time, I applied via my congressman for an appointment to the U.S. Naval Academy in Annapolis, MD.

I was approved for the Naval Academy but I had already accepted the NROTC scholarship. At the time, I had no plans to make a career in the Navy so I opted for the NROTC program.

Had I accepted my appointment to the Academy, I suppose it might have been advantageous in the long run to my Navy career which I did end up pursuing. In the Academy, one tends to pick up mentors who can help with matters pertaining to career sponsorship. Those mentors tend to be Flag Officers (or Admirals). Still, I did pick up some important mentors some of which were junior to me during my career progression. I am not sure I really ever needed mentorship.

I have always tended to be rather adventurous. For that reason, after having served two successful tours afloat, I volunteered for potentially hazardous duty in-country Vietnam as an advisor to the South Vietnamese Naval forces operating around the Mekong River. A senior mentor would probably have advised against that in as much as the War at that time was winding down and becoming less attractive on a resume. Furthermore, I later volunteered to be an exchange officer with the Navy of Argentina. A senior mentor would have advised me against that because it was too far outside the mainstream of the U.S. Navy. No one could see the Falkland War coming. Finally, towards the end of my career when I was serving on the Chief of Naval Operations Staff with responsibility for administrating a three-billion-dollar program of military sales to Spain as that country was entering NATO. I became aware of an attaché position opening up in Madrid. The timing was right in terms of my rotation so I requested consideration for the position. During a business trip to Spain, I paid a call on the American Ambassador at the embassy. I had already established a good working relationship with the Ambassador. I told him I would like to be a member of his diplomatic team and he readily agreed. I asked him to make a by-name request for me via State Department channels which he did. An effective mentor would veto that idea because I was technically going outside Navy channels to get it. A mentor would have pointed out the potential for career suicide. On the upside, as an attaché, I was awarded the Defense Superior Service medal and I was cited for being the most prolific intelligence reporter among my attaché group. In spite of my getting the job and performing it very well, the Bureau of Personnel took a dim view of my initiative. I did not regard myself as just being another brick in the wall. I was more proactive than that when it came to pursuing positions I wanted.

Among my best choices in my career was to learn two languages fluently besides English: Vietnamese and Spanish. When you learn another language, you gain assets in terms of insights and learning how to think thoughts you can't think otherwise. This was of central importance to me in terms of understanding the cultures I was operating in. I am not sure any mentor would have adequately understood this.

For example, in Vietnam I learned they have a much more elastic concept of time. Their sense of past and present is blurred compared to ours. "I go" and "I went" mean about the same thing. If one means to specify one went and that action is now over and complete, one can add a special word to clarify. That can amount to a lot of misunderstanding when it comes to a question like "Did you conduct a patrol?" If the answer is yes you may need to ask when. If the answer is yesterday you have narrowed down the concept to what I was used to as a Westerner. If the answer is tomorrow, I needed additional clarification. This forced me to realize that I needed to think in the present tense and then deduce the true concept of time I was used to dealing with.

In Spain and to a lesser extent in Argentine culture, heritage is destiny. If you were a male born to a naval officer, you were destined to be a naval officer, too. As a pre-teen, you would be enrolled into the Liceo Naval, a prep school for the Spanish Naval Academy where you would be educated and trained to be a naval officer from the ground up. That would include Spanish naval history, basic seamanship, academic studies, physical education and other skills you would need to progress and build upon.

I personally knew several Spanish naval officers who were descended from as many as thirteen unbroken generations of naval officer forbearers. One such officer had an ancestor who commanded a Spanish ship during the Battle of Pensacola Bay, a little-known battle during the American Revolution when the Spanish fleet was operating with the French fleet in support of our revolution.

Another interesting thing about the Spanish Navy is that they always have a Christopher Columbus as an admiral on active duty. When that admiral dies, the next direct descendent of Christopher Columbus changes his name to Cristobal Colon (Christopher Columbus in English) and assumes all the hereditary rights and titles pertaining to the name, e.g., a Duke. If not already a flag officer he will be destined to become one. I made rank on time throughout my career so I guess I was successful by that measure. I spent way more than my fair share of duty at sea. Basically, I had a great and wonderfully interesting career based upon my own stewardship. I was not destined to be an admiral as will become evident as you read my book. I loved the U.S. Navy nonetheless.

A KENTUCKY BOY GOES TO SEA AS A NAVAL OFFICER

CHAPTER 1

Early Immersion into the Navy

F irst Liberty Call—I was twenty years old. It was 1965. I was a Navy midshipman 3rd class (officer trainee). Part of my training involved participation in three summer-long training cruises. My first such cruise was on an old straight decked aircraft carrier of WWII vintage, USS *Lake Champlain* (CVS—57). She was commissioned just a bit too late to participate in WWII. Her factitious nickname was the "straightest and the greatest." Her main mission was anti-submarine warfare. She carried a variety of helicopters most of which were equipped with dipping sonars. As well, a wing of S-2F tracker fixed-wing two engine propeller-driven aircraft called "Stoofs" were typically embarked. The Stoofs could carry two acoustic homing torpedoes for use against submarines plus numerous sonobuoys the Stoofs could deploy and then monitor. My rank in terms of hierarchy was like whale shit at the bottom of the ocean.

As a result of her older design, the USS *Lake Champlain* had an open bow structure as opposed to an enclosed, more protected "hurricane" bow more common to the newer aircraft carriers. One could walk to the frontmost part of the open bow under the flight deck and look down to the stem of the ship cutting through the water as she moved forward. If one looked up, a sizable hole was evident in one of the I-beams under the flight deck. I had no idea water under pressure could pierce the web of a steel beam but there was the proof. The damage had occurred some years earlier while the ship was operating at sea during foul weather. The damage was judged as operationally inconsequential and was never fully repaired.

As I looked down from that vantage point while the ship was operating at nearly full power in the Chesapeake Bay, I was surprised to see a large hammerhead shark near the surface. It passed under the ship.

While we midshipmen were embarked, we got to take rides in the S-2F trackers. Our aircraft were launched from the bow with steam catapults. Being a straight decked carrier, and if the aircraft was not properly powered up during launch, it would go into the water dead ahead of the ship and then the ship would run over the aircraft as if it were the large hammerhead shark I had observed.

When we landed on the carrier during our familiarization flights, the aircraft caught an arresting wire. That was a memorable experience. I was sure we had crashed. I could see the various shock mounted equipment moving around on their mountings.

After our operations in the Chesapeake Bay and in the nearby Atlantic, the ship pulled into New York City for a few days of liberty. It was my first visit there. We were wearing civilian clothing as opposed to the rather inappropriate-for-use-ashore midshipmen uniforms we wore at sea. A popular drink in those days was the Singapore Sling which we assiduously sought out in the bars of New York City.

I remember the awful berthing compartment where my colleagues and I were assigned. It was directly under the old wood flight deck through which I could see stars twinkling at night between the openings in the old wood decking of the flight deck. If it rained, we got wet. When planes landed or launched above us, we were jolted from our stacked bunks. The unsettling thought occurred that spilled aviation fuel could find its way to us if a flight deck disaster might happen.

Naval Officer Reserve Training Corps midshipmen arrived at the ship before a larger group of Naval Academy midshipmen who had been drinking before coming aboard. Being from the academy they had not much experience drinking. The latter group had to pass through our berthing compartment to get to theirs. The academy midshipmen did not like us. A bottleneck developed at a narrow water-tight door in our compartment. Tempers flared and a fight broke out between the NROTC types and the Naval Academy types. A friend of mine, a large Miami University Redskin varsity football player of Hungarian extraction tried to step in and make peace but was punched. Bad, bad mistake. The naval academy guys caught the worst end of the deal by far.

The aim of our first training cruise was to familiarize us with the enlisted way of life. Mostly we performed slave labor such as bilge cleaning during our time aboard. We performed work self-respecting sailors disdained or we stood various engineering watches in the fire rooms (think boilers) or noisy engine rooms. The snipes (boiler techs, enginemen or machinist mates) hazed us without mercy. We weren't yet officers and were therefore sort of fair game for harassment by the enlisted snipes.

We wore a version of the enlisted navy uniform except for our dixie cup sailor hats which had a blue stripe towards the top of the hat. The enlisted crew members spread rumors to women ashore to the effect the blue stripe signified venereal disease.

One evening I was standing watch in one of the engine rooms alongside a petty officer. Another unseen fireman shot a salt pill at me with a peashooter. In those days, salt pill dispensers were located throughout the sweltering engineering spaces of the ship. Whap! The salt pill hit me with considerable force on my neck. The petty officer seemed to sympathize with me. He told me to fill a bucket with water. Then he gave me some rather complicated directions that involved going up and down ladders and around various machinery equipment. He told me if I followed his directions carefully, I would find myself a deck above my tormentor where I could dump my bucket of water upon him. I did as he said but when I finally got there my tormentor was not where he was supposed to be. He was a deck above me. He dumped a bucket of water on me. It was impossible for me to maintain any dignity at all.

The Navy has a serious fascination with boxing events called smokers. I remember that one particular sailor, a member of the crew, was very skilled as a boxer. He was a serious contender at the fleet level. While we were at sea aboard the *Lake Champlain*, we midshipmen participated in a smoker. We boxed against other fellow midshipmen in the hangar bay. I do not think any of us midshipmen covered ourselves in glory. We had no finesse and did not bob and weave to any real degree. We simply slugged one another senseless.

We also watched movies in the hangar bay after the evening meal at sea. I remember seeing the movie *Cleopatra* starring Elizabeth Taylor and Richard Burton. It was a new release.

The ship was home ported at Quonset Point near Newport, Rhode Island. By fortuitous circumstance, the annual Newport Jazz Festival was in full swing. I enjoyed that greatly and I remember the musician Dizzy Gillespie in particular. We were quick to learn that nobody ashore carded us including the Newport package stores.

One weekend when we did not have duty, another midshipman fool and I decided to check out Cape Cod which neither of us had ever visited. I don't remember how we got there but I do remember finding an impromptu band and a party on a beach in the Falmouth area. The band was using a loud generator to power their musical equipment and had to turn up their amplifiers for the music to be heard over the loud generator. Later that rainy night, my friend and I sought shelter in a nearby baseball field dug-out.

As my other fool colleague and I sat on our bench in the dug-out we noticed an attractive young woman wandering around on the baseball field in the drizzling rain. She apparently failed to take notice of us because she dropped her pants and peed on the home plate. We were close witnesses. After a short polite interlude, I called to her and invited her to share our meager shelter and a pint of Myer's Dark Rum which I had illicitly scored from a Newport package store. Obviously embarrassed and mortified, she nonetheless decided to accept our hospitality and passed much of the evening in pleasant social discourse with us. Looking back, that is the most remarkable memory of my real liberty runs ashore. It set the tone for many, many such runs ashore during my 21-year career in the Navy.

The second-class midshipman training cruise came between our second and third year of college. It consisted of two phases: the first phase was basic naval aviation training at the Naval Air Station in Corpus Christi, Texas. We were given classroom instruction, homework study assignments and supervised instruction in the tandem seat aircraft where the instructor pilot had a good view of his students. As I recall, it was the T2 piston driven air craft we trained in. I had been randomly selected to be a company commander of the midshipmen. Unfortunately, that duty took my attention away from the homework assignments. I was ill prepared and sleepy the next morning and had to ask my instructor pilot to guide me through the process of starting the plane and taking it down the runway. My instructor was not very impressed with me.

Both phases of the training involved considerable physical training as well as daily marching drills. The second phase of the second training cruise had us in the amphibious navy and took place at the Navy Amphibious Base at Little Creek in Virginia. The culmination of that training towards the end of our cruise had us embarked on an older, cramped personnel transport. We constituted an amphibious landing force. We slept in stacked bunks only inches apart vertically and laterally. Our rifles were secured to the side of our bunks.

We scrambled over the side of the ship by climbing down rope netting into bobbing and swaying LCVP (Landing Craft Vehicle & Personnel) amphibious craft idling next to the troop ship. We were carrying full packs and rifles. One of my colleagues slipped on the way down the net and was suspended upside down by his ankle over the LCVP. Someone managed to free his foot and he fell into the craft but he did that with class. He landed on his feet and smiled at us. He was lucky. He could have broken his neck.

The various landing craft milled around in circles off the beach long enough to get many of us sea sick. Then, we arrived at the beach and the landing craft bow gate opened and fell down into the surf. We waded in through the water and once ashore we assaulted our objective area of the beach which had pill boxes and other fortifications. Our M1 rifles were loaded with blanks.

After our assault, we were herded into bleachers where we observed the second wave of troops landing. Those troops, active-duty marines were there to show us how it was supposed to go. They stormed ashore with real weapons and munitions including satchel charges. They blew up several bunkers. It was all very authentic. I'm unaware of any of us being seriously injured during the training.

For a strenuous couple of days, we were introduced to special warfare frogman training. At that time frogmen were UDT (Underwater Demolition Team) members as opposed to the later SEAL (Sea Air Land) designation. Our brief indoctrination mostly consisted of beach training. We were assigned six-man rubber boats operating and racing in the surf. I remember the boat I was in leaked badly. In spite of that handicap, we managed not to come in last in the races. Maybe the last boat in the race leaked worse than our craft.

Our third and final training cruise had an objective aimed at introducing us to the duties and the life of junior officers aboard ships, mostly destroyers. It came during our junior year of college. We wore uniforms that were closer to making us look like officers.

Smaller contingents of us first class midshipmen were assigned to destroyers. I was assigned to USS *Steinaker* (DD-863), a Gearing Class destroyer, based in Norfolk, Virginia.

We occupied officer berthing quarters and we were served meals in the wardroom with the officers of the ship. In port, we stood quarterdeck watches as officers of the deck under instruction where we were trained in matters of traditional protocol such as rendering proper honors to visiting or embarked senior officers. We were also trained as boat officers in that we learned how to supervise the boat crews, how to navigate the boats in harbors, how to properly render passing honors, etc. We also learned from practical exercises about operating anchoring equipment and how to properly moor or anchor a ship.

At sea, we stood various watches such as Junior Officer of the Deck or in the Combat Information Center (CIC) under-instruction, where we studied basics relating to maneuvering the ship and Junior Engineer Officer of the Watch in the engine room. Further, we rotated around enlisted watch stander stations learning about what signalmen and a variety of other watch standers do including look-outs, helmsmen, etc. At the same time, we followed certain officers around such as the Navigator, Anti-Submarine Warfare (ASW) officer or the Gunnery Officers to become familiar with what they did on a daily basis. Sometimes we functioned as messengers for officers.

A friend recently asked me why I chose the Navy over other services. Truth is, the Navy chose me more than I chose it. A high school guidance counselor told me about a Navy scholarship program which she thought would be a good fit for me. I agreed and I applied for the scholarship.

The testing, both physically and scholastically was very challenging. I also had to undergo a thorough security screening process by the Federal Bureau of Investigation. If I were successful in becoming a midshipman it would eventually lead to a commission as a regular Navy or Marine Corps officer as opposed to a reserve officer. I decided to pursue a Navy commission and was very hopeful for the NROTC scholarship. I managed to pass all of the hurdles and I got a full ride: tuition, books and even a modest cash allowance for incidentals (beer mostly). The Navy was the only service that offered such a good deal. Conditions of the scholarship were rather ample. I was prohibited from majoring in certain areas not related to the Navy such as architecture. I also had to go to school where the Navy sent me: Miami University in Ohio. This was okay with me since I was familiar with that fine institution. While the process of testing and security clearance worked itself out, I also applied to the U.S. Naval Academy in Annapolis via my congressman. I was nominated for the Academy but as first alternate. Turns out the guy ahead of me flunked his physical exam and I became the primary nominee. By then I had decided to go with the NROTC scholarship. At the time, I had no intentions of making the Navy a career. That decision came some years later.

I became a member of the NROTC unit at Miami University in Oxford, Ohio, along with about sixty other midshipmen in my class. About half of us were Regular Midshipmen meaning we were recipients of full scholarships while the remainder were Contract or reserve students eligible for a reserve commission upon graduation. The NROTC unit was organized as a battalion. The unit also had a lesser number of enlisted Navy and Marine members who were selected from the ranks to pursue commissions upon graduation. Those members did not drill with us midshipmen nor were they referred to as midshipmen. They were referred to as NESEPs (Navy Enlisted Science Education Program). They typically did not wear uniforms nor did they study the naval courses required of midshipmen. They mostly studied pure science courses of study. I imagine the NESEPs probably were sent to "knife and fork" finishing school for final training before commissioning. The midshipmen wore uniforms once a week and drilled on the same day.

I basically pursued a liberal arts education. Early on I was accepted into an honors creative writing program and majored in

My Commissioning Ceremony as Ensign, U.S. Navy, at Miami University, 1968. *Left to right*: Charles (father), Betty Ann (mother), Ensign Hall, Michael (younger brother), Tony (youngest brother)

English. I also studied psychology which was interesting to me as well as trigonometry. Further, I studied Naval Science including navigation, propulsion engineering, naval history and weapons not to mention a variety of other academic electives. The Naval Science courses were taught by Navy or Marine officers on the NROTC staff. I was later surprised to learn NROTC graduates had a higher retention rate than our Naval Academy colleagues. My academic experience at Miami University was spotty because I was not very focused at first. For the first two years, my grades were mediocre. They got better as I went along. By my senior year I was getting straight A's.

A KENTUCKY BOY GOES TO SEA AS A NAVAL OFFICER

CHAPTER 2

My Roots

I was born and raised in a hollow of the mystical iron ore and coal-infused hills of eastern Kentucky. I have ancestors who came into Kentucky with the first party of white settlers led there by Daniel Boone. My ancestry is primarily of Scottish and German stock but DNA analysis suggests I have some Melungeon make-up as well. Melungeons are a tri-racial people who are mostly found in Kentucky and Tennessee. They are a mix of Cherokee, Black and Caucasian blood. Notable people with Melungeon ancestry include Abraham Lincoln and Elvis Presley. Big boned bodies, gray eyes and darker skin tend to be common Melungeon characteristics.

My cousin, Jesse Stuart, was a famed, prolific writer and poet laureate of the Commonwealth of Kentucky. He made his place in literary history when I was a young boy. As a writer he was in the class and company of Hemingway and Steinbeck, particularly in the short story genre. Some of his works such as the novel *The Thread that Runs So True* were required reading when I was in high school.

Jesse Stuart also published a notable short story about Melungeons in which he detailed the life and death of a female moonshiner. Revenue officers arrested her but could not apprehend her because she had grown too large to fit through the door of her cabin. They had to settle for destroying her still which she simply rebuilt and then shortly thereafter resumed her moonshining career. When she died, her family was forced to knock down the chimney of her home in order to make an opening large enough to extricate her body for burial. Jesse Stuart was known for writing stories based on some degree of truth. The story was published as *Sylvania is Dead.*

Most of my people were not as prominent as Jesse Stuart. They tended to be farmers and coal miner types on both sides of my lineage. An uncle on my paternal side of the family, whose early education was in one-room schoolhouses, was the first to go to college. He graduated from Berea College in Kentucky. I was the second when I won my scholarship to Miami University.

My family had a distinct military heritage. I ended up following it. Like many Kentuckians I have ancestors who fought on both sides in the War Between the States. Two great grandfathers were German mercenaries imported to fight for the Union side. A grand uncle, Carl Ossendott, served in the Army in the Philippines and then later in WWI. He was gassed somewhere on a battlefield in Europe and began a long and lingering mental and physical deterioration that ended with him living and dying with my paternal grandparents. He is buried in the Hall family cemetery on what was then the farm of my paternal grandfather, Charles W. Hall, Sr.

My maternal grandfather, Carl Bustetter, was in the Texas Cavalry for some years up until the time when it was disbanded. He served in Texas under General "Black Jack" Pershing chasing but never catching Pancho Villa as Villa conducted his nefarious raids around the Texas border areas. He returned to Kentucky after his service discharge, worked as a barber and in other capacities. He then purchased and cleared a sizable farm and planted and managed 72 acres of apple, peach, pear and plum orchards plus a sizable vineyard as well as significant plantings of sweet potatoes, corn, watermelons and such. He basically worked himself to death but before he died, he was a big influence on me. He loved and owned horses and mules and he taught me to ride.

My father, Charles Hall, Jr., was a skinny Kentucky farm kid who joined the Army before WWII. He was inducted into the Army Air Corps and became an enlisted pilot. He gained some fame in the local community because he would fly a small aircraft from somewhere in Ohio to the family farm in Eastern Kentucky where he would drop packages for his younger brother into a field near the farm house. The packages contained clothing, candy and such.

My father was then sent on a sweltering, slow transport ship to Clark Air Base in the Philippines. He was a B-17 tail gunner and later bombardier. Lucky for him, his flight group was transferred to Hickam Air Base in Hawaii before the War broke out. Had he remained in the Philippines he would likely have been captured by the Japanese and would have been subjected to the infamous Bataan Death March. Unlucky for him, he was at Hickam Air Base during the Pearl Harbor attack. He was wounded by a bomb fragment doing damage to a hand during the attack but he recovered fairly quickly. He qualified for humanitarian leave over the Christmas holiday season, as a result of his wound and by some means found his way back to Eastern Kentucky.

He wrote to his parents about his upcoming leave and his planned return home. Apparently, the Pearl Harbor attack and the War in general had disrupted a lot of things including postal mail service. His letter never arrived at his parents home before he did. My grandparents must have been very worried about his status.

Meanwhile, another Kentucky boy from the same local area had been stationed at Hickam Air Base in another unit at the same time as my father was there. The other boy had established renewed contact with my father before the attack. Following the Japanese attack, he had wandered around the airbase where he encountered a corpse clad in the uniform of an Army Air Corps airman. The corpse apparently looked as though he were my father in terms of height and other physical characteristics including rank insignia but the other boy lacked the courage or presence of mind to turn the body over and make sure it was in fact my father.

The other boy was also granted compassionate leave at about the same time as my father. Upon return home he sought out the Presbyterian minister who served the church attended by my family members. He told the minister he was fairly sure my father had been killed in the attack. The minister forthwith made plans to visit my grandparents so as to console them.

My Mammaw takes over the narrative at this point. I heard her narrative many times and I never tired of it. She told me the minister had arrived at their farmhouse when a bus pulled up near the house very shortly thereafter. My father, wearing his uniform descended from the bus with his bag. He stepped off the bus and into the warm embrace of his mother. My Mammaw was a very religious person. She read a lot into the timing of her re-encounter with her prodigal son and the almost simultaneous visit of the minister. She had some significant spiritual avenues to contemplate during that Christmas holiday season which was likely the best of her life.

This is my memoir and not that of my Mammaw nor of my father nor anyone else. I was not yet born when many of the events described above happened. Notwithstanding, I see myself as a mere single point in my family continuum, past and present. Family members went before me and others followed me but from the time they began to arrive in Kentucky to the present, they all come together to define me as an end product of a process. All of them made me the Kentuckian that I am. That's about the only way to understand me because that was how I was built. In other words, I am not a person who bumbled around amid and among the detritus of my heritage as I tried to decide who or what I am. That is a matter already decided. This is a very southern kind of sentiment and ethic and it has flavored the substance of my life. I am defined as a Kentuckian by the Commonwealth of Kentucky itself even though I no longer reside there.

My father was subsequently involved in more than four years of continued and fierce aerial combat in the Pacific theater of operations including the Solomon and Marianas Islands campaigns as well as others. He was offered an assignment to an unspecified but top secret program which he declined. He later deduced that program might have been the Manhattan Project for the development of an atomic weapon. After the War, he returned to Kentucky, married my mother, who was a true and classic Kentucky beauty, and began a very successful career from the bottom up in the steel industry. He eventually progressed to being the National Transportation Manager of Armco Steel Company which was a large prestigious leader in the steel industry at that time.

I am the eldest of his three children, all boys. As mentioned before, I obtained a Navy scholarship and that led to a 21-year career as a surface warfare officer. My next oldest brother served a four-year hitch as an enlisted Marine and served a tour in-country Vietnam. Later he served for several years in the Merchant Marine and saw a lot of commercial sea service. My youngest brother became an Air Force pilot flying KC-135 tanker aircraft. He served several years including during the Gulf War. He later had a long career as an American Airlines Captain.

Extremely important to my formation was my paternal grandmother: my Mammaw, Ona (Onie) Ossendott Hall. She was an amazing woman. Not formally educated, she was a true empath: she just knew things sometimes on seemingly a supernatural level. Just a casual walk with her around her farm was a multi-faceted education every time. She knew how to get into your head and teach, teach, teach. I can't picture her without her constant apron which she always wore except when dressed for church.

The modest Hall farm was quite self-sufficient. Our main crops were corn and tobacco. We had a few live stock (cows and a draft horse for plowing) plus some pigs and lots of chickens. We also had a smokehouse that produced a large amount of bacon, hams and such. Under the smokehouse was a root cellar with an uncountable number of mason jars to hold the bounty of produce from a large garden. We even had our own coal mine on our property to serve all our heating, cooking and fire place needs. The mine was

"The Hall Homestead in Eastern Kentucky,"
an oil painting by the author

really just an exposed vein of coal on a hillside cliff not far from the house, It got deeper into the hill the more we dug into it.

We churned our own butter. Churning butter was my first assigned chore as a child. Later, as I grew a bit older, I was upgraded to the more elevated status of chicken killer. That was mildly challenging for when I first chopped the chicken head off of a chicken with an axe, it seemed to be headlessly chasing me in an ever decreasing circle. Fortunately, my young uncle had already and effectively exposed me to that aspect of chicken killing and I got over it quickly. We feasted on fried chicken on most Sundays, so I was busy as a chicken killer.

An early enduring memory of mine was when I slept in a small bunk house near the main house. The bunk house was located under a very large cherry tree. I would be awakened by the sound of cherry pits pelting the tin roof of the bunk house as birds fed upon the cherries. It was like music to my ears. Another enduring memory was that of home made peach ice cream. We would put dry-ice purchased from a gas station down the road into an ice cream maker and I would grind the machine until my young arms could no longer turn the handle any more as the ice cream began to thicken. Then a stronger adult such as one of my uncles, my father or perhaps my Pappaw would take over until the best ice cream in the world was ready to serve. Enjoyment was enhanced by my aching arms, being able to observe from close at hand both the cow that gave the cream and the peach tree from which the peaches had been picked.

The dwelling was a comfortable modest farmhouse with lots of room inside. Being serviced by an out-house for a sanitary waste system, it had scant indoor plumbing: only the kitchen sink involved plumbing and that was only for drainage. It was built over a large open crawlspace which was home to innumerable and unnamed cats which were close to being feral. Sweet tasting water came from a dug well in the back yard. I have since learned the best water in the country is from Kentucky and New York State. No wonder Kentucky is famous for distilling bourbon whiskey.

Not until the late 1940s did we have luxury things like electricity or motor vehicles. To get where we wanted to go, which was never far, we relied on a velocipede. A velocipede is an old type of rail-road hand car that had to be placed on the rail road tracks that went by the farm. Then, a couple of men or boys would propel the thing by pumping the see-saw contraption on the car.

My grandmother, or Mammaw, was the moral authority and leader of everything to do with life on the Hall farm. Her husband, my grandfather, or Pappaw, ceded that to her. He was the hard worker while she was the otherwise constant beating heart of the family.

My grandmother lost her 15-year-old son, my uncle Carl, to scarlet fever before I was born. He was subsequently buried within sight of her farmhouse in our family cemetery. She saw his gravestone every day. Her grief proved almost unbearable. She went into a deep clinical depression for some years. No Christmas nor any other holiday was celebrated during that time. Family legend has it that she even dug up his grave once to see him one more time and to put some mementos with him.

I am told and I believe when I was born, I constituted the therapy that snapped her out of her mental illness. My parents moved us in to live with her on the farm perhaps out of design for that therapy or perhaps they just needed a place to live when my father returned from the War and married my mother. In any case, I was her first grandchild and she doted on and spoiled me relentlessly. She was a prodigious baker of pies and cakes. The tempo of life in the house revolved around her coal-fired stove and oven which was stoked early in the morning. By mid-day it was ready for the main mid-day meal. By late afternoon it was perfect for baking. My grandmother made corn bread every day without fail. My Pappaw ate corn-bread for his evening meal without fail. His last chore of the day was that of milking our one or two cows. He would then seat himself at the dining table, remove his dentures which he placed on the table next to his bowl and then pour warm milk fresh from the cow over warm corn bread and enjoy. Aside from corn bread, whatever else Mammaw baked: pies and cakes of all kinds, she always baked one more just for me. That went on for years. She talked to me constantly and I was always at her side even before I can remember being so. I think I must have imprinted her into my soul.

As I said, she was an empath. She knew everything that was in my little head as well as many other heads. Later, when I was a bit older, she tried to convince me to be a sissy. She had become sick and tired of war given what every generation she knew had gone through from the War Between the States, WWI and WWII. She did not want me to be in any war. I rejected that advice and went on to my war in Vietnam but to this day her anti-war advice resounds.

As a youngster, I had a mischievous streak which frequently got me in trouble. One day my younger brother and I were playing in our backyard. I talked my brother into playing a prank on my mother who was poised to look out of a kitchen window as she was washing dishes at the sink. The prank consisted of me tying a loop of rope under my brother's arms pits and then putting his coat on over the rope to conceal it. Then, I hoisted him up to an oak tree limb overhanging the backyard. Next, I told him to cross his eyes, stick out his tongue and hold the pose.

I went into the kitchen and pointed out to my mother the spectacle of my brother swinging from the tree by a rope. I observed a phenomenon I had never seen before. I saw her heart apparently trying to get out of her chest. That scared me and I awkwardly helped her to a chair as I lamely attempted to explain it away as a prank.

Another example of my mischievousness was when I put a water hose into one of my grandfather's bee hives. I turned the water on which produced a swarm of angry bees. A cousin then agitatedly ran through the swarm cursing and yelling as he endured a number of stings.

We rebel Kentucky children considered it high sport to attach transparent monofilament fishing line to an old wallet or purse, perhaps with a stapled dollar bill sticking out for enhanced bait, and then place it in the middle of a road while we hid out of sight. Cars or trucks would stop to examine the lure. We would wait until the occupant of the vehicle got out of the vehicle and close to the item then we would jerk the item away from them. A surprising number of our victims would chase the item.

Sometimes around Halloween we would tie a line to a tree limb overhanging an inclined roadway and around a cat on the other end of the line. We would then wait for dark when vehicles turned on their headlights. As the vehicle came up the incline with its lights on, we would let go of the cat which would swing splay-footed into the light beams and then over the vehicle as if it were flying. Looking back, I am not proud of having participated in this rather cruel prank. I eventually grew up.

At times, I seemed to be prone to accidents as was the case when I was searching for fishing bait late one summer when worms were down deep in the soil and scarce. The thought occurred that wasp larvae would suit my needs. So, I climbed up high in the rafters of my grandfather's tobacco barn with a torch of newspapers. I proceeded to burn the wings off of the wasps that were clinging to the paper wasp nest then I would put the nests into my pocket. The adult wasps dropped harmlessly to the floor of the barn. I got sloppy and positioned myself under a nest when I was burning the wings off wasps above me. The wingless wasps fell inside my shirt and proceeded to sting me. Wasps typically do not simply sting once but instead repeatedly. The pain was great but I could not take my hands off the rafters without risking a fall from up high. I had to simply grit my teeth and hold on.

I was nine years old when my father gave me my first gun. It was a little Sears J.C. Higgins single shot .410 gauge shot gun. My father attached strict conditions to my ownership of the gun aside from keeping it gleamingly clean, well-oiled and polished with linseed oil on the wood parts.

First, he pledged me not to ride motor cycles. He had a thing about motor cycles. Being very eager to get the gun, I rather quickly agreed to the pledge. I have ended up honoring that pledge during my long life of 75 years to date.

Second, he told me I would not be allowed ammunition for the gun until I proved I was utterly safe to carry a loaded weapon. In the meantime, I carried the gun unloaded in the field with him. He critiqued me without mercy especially when he observed me crossing fences or when I lagged behind him in the field. He judged those circumstances to be the most dangerous situations for a neophyte young hunter. He watched me like a hawk.

I was taught to break the action on my gun upon approaching a fence and then to climb over the fence, preferably at a fence stile, before reaching back across the fence for it. Only then could I snap the gun action back into place. I was further taught to always keep abreast of my hunting companions in the field so as to keep aware of where they were.

There was wisdom in his strict requirements. He did not want me to do two things at once in crossing a fence: climb over the fence and safely handle a gun at the same time. The rabbits and quail that were our usual quarry often bedded down in the vegetation adjacent to a fence. If the prey flushed at such a point in time the young hunter might be tempted to go after the prey instead of doing the safe thing. Better to let the rabbit or bird go. Further, if I were to lag too far behind my colleague, I might swing my gun towards them when I was too eager to follow a target going in their direction.

I also hunted squirrels assiduously. To a lesser degree I hunted opossums. Pursuit of both, was mostly a solitary and pleasant stalking endeavor. My grandmother was a wonderful cook and squirrels have a meat that is deliciously aromatic when being cooked or fried. Squirrel and dumplings remains one of my favorite dishes to this day but I rarely get to enjoy it.

When I was young, deer and wild turkey had long since disappeared from Kentucky maybe due to the extensive loss of habitat due to wide-spread and destructive strip mining practices that were ruining the Kentucky landscape. The deer and turkey came back later but not while I was a young boy hunting in the hills. Today, deer and turkey have returned to Kentucky in strength. I have learned to hunt them but I never learned that there.

Finally, after undergoing his relentless scrutiny for what seemed forever my father judged me as provisionally worthy. One evening he gave me a pocketful of shot gun shells the night before a hunt on my grandparent's Eastern Kentucky farm.

Early the next morning, my Mammaw Hall prepared a big hearty breakfast of biscuits and gravy for the hunting party which consisted of my Papaw, my father, an uncle and me. As we prepared for a day of hunting, everyone got up from the kitchen table. My Mammaw decided I needed a second helping of breakfast and she put it in front of me. My father told me to meet them "beyond the gate" when I finished. I had always been told if I was not ten minutes early for anything, I was late. I decided I would eat my second helping of breakfast.

After I finished, I got my shotgun and walked through the large vegetable garden behind the house towards the gate at the other end of the garden. Awaiting me there were my Papaw, my father, my uncle and a rather over-weight beagle hound that could not wait to hunt. The dog was borrowed from a neighbor. We always had dogs but for some reason at that time we did not.

I was not chastised for holding them up. They all knew my Mammaw doted on me and they forgave me for being slightly late. None of them would challenge Mammaw on any subject. The pleasant memory and images of walking through that garden and then through the gate somehow stuck with me for years. Everything was covered in frost just like in the lyrics of the song "Dixie."

We proceeded into the fields. I will always remember three small screech owls, apparently young fledglings, sitting in a row on the limb of a tree. They stared at us with big curious eyes without flying away. We returned their intense gaze. I do not remember any more specific details about the hunt but I do remember we rarely returned empty handed with nothing in our game pouches.

Years later I was a young naval officer serving on the rivers and coastal areas of Vietnam. I was unsure if I would survive my dangerous duties. During difficult times when I could neither sleep nor eat well, I began to burnish and polish what had been this pleasant memory into a cherished keepsake of my life. I even began to hope when I died my spirit would be allowed enough spiritual sentience to walk through my Mammaw's garden and then through a gate at the far end to whatever waited which I hoped would be among my kin and a dog that could not wait to hunt.

Fishing with my father: I am and always have been an avid angler. I mostly fly fish these days and I tie my own flies. That is my pinnacle as a seventy-five-year-old fisherman. My father introduced me to fishing probably before I was five years old. But back then it wasn't about fly rods or even hooks and line. It was called "noodling" back in Eastern Kentucky but I do not recall my father calling it that. He referred to it as the "Indian Way of Fishing." We fished in East Fork Creek, a medium sized estuary that ran past our farm. Of particular interest were bank-side trees with roots that reached into the water. In June, catfish congregate in such places to mate. He had me get my hands cold enough in the creek before slipping them into the undercuts and roots and then feeling for the catfish. It was like using braille. You had to use touch as opposed to vision. He coached me to slip a finger or two into the gills and then pull out and flip the fish onto the bank. His only warning was that if I found legs and claws: leave it be. That was a snapping turtle.

Looking back, that was the best way to start my fishing career. Up close, intimate and touchy-feely. It was real that way. Later, we progressed to rod, hook, line and worm fishing, Then one day he had me stand on the creek bed while he waded into the water in front of me. That area of the bottom of the creek was covered with fallen sunken leaves. He began to scoop up the mud and throw it towards me. Lots of eels were squirming in what he threw towards me. I picked the slippery things up and put them into a bait container. They were the best bass bait in the world. What a revelation!

My father also taught me how to catch suckers with cornmeal-based dough bait. Suckers can grow to good size but in general were not sought after except perhaps during the depression era when nothing was wasted. They are very bony, but my grandmother knew how to prepare them. I would fillet them and she would marinate the fillets over-night in vinegar which dissolved the bones. Before breading and frying them, she would wash off the vinegar. They were culinary delights with no taste of vinegar at all. One day, I began throwing a small spoon lure into a shallow pool of the creek. For some reason, my father had never regarded that pool as potentially productive. I came away with a very nice stringer of small mouth bass and my father was quite impressed. I was teaching my master a thing or two.

My father progressed in fishing as well over his life. He had a good job as a steel company executive that started with a managerial position with Armco Steel in Ashland, Kentucky and in his senior years he fished all over the world. Tarpon and sailfish in Central America. After he retired, he moved to Florida and bought a sizable fishing boat. I fished with him whenever I could. Both of us got into fly fishing as well. We were never closer than when fishing or talking about fishing. My typical Christmas gift to him was some sort of book about fishing.

It all started when he had me fishing the "Indian Way" in a Kentucky creek. I haven't done that again but maybe I have to before I get too old. I'm going fishing for trout with some old friends again next month in the Smokey Mountains. Maybe, I'll give it another shot. I know some places where I might try and I know it works on trout because the Indians proved it.

I was close to my father for the duration of his life although there were times our relationship was strained. We always mended our fences by going fishing. Then everything was right again. This continued to be our way of getting along until he died by suicide in the late 1990s when he could no longer deal with his congestive heart disease diagnosis and its complications.

He tried to get me into golf but it was always about fishing and hunting which both of us were good at. By then, he lived in Florida. I think he may have bought that boat in the hope it would draw me to him. My two brothers never got much into hunting and fishing like I did. That boat may have been kind of a monument to our father-son love for fishing and for one another.

To this day, I am an avid fisherman. Every time I go fishing my father is there. We compete to some degree. My daughters now fly fish with me from time to time. I like to think my father is somewhere near us when we go on the water.

CHAPTER 3

Early Sea Duty on USS *Laffey* (DD-724) in Her Later Years

I graduated from Miami University in 1968 when Vietnam was heating up. I was commissioned as an Ensign, U.S. Navy with orders to USS *Laffey* (DD-724) based in Norfolk, Virginia. Many of my classmates requested aviation duty. Even though I passed the daunting physical tests for flight duty, I opted for duty in the surface navy for several reasons.

First of all, the aviators incurred a longer mandatory service requirement mostly because flight training was rather long. At the time, I had no aspirations for a career in the Navy and therefore wanted to keep my options open in terms of leaving the Navy after four years. Second, unlike some of my classmates, I did not have any fire in my belly for flying. About 20 percent of naval aviators would die in flight-related accidents or combat action and I figured if I did not have the fire in the belly, I would probably be a casualty. Finally, I am a traditionalist at heart. I tended to like the idea of traditional sea service. I liked ships and the prospect of working with the sailors on them.

Before reporting to the *Laffey*, I went to Key West, Florida where I attended six weeks of Anti-Submarine Officer Training at the Fleet Sonar School. This was to prepare me for the job of Anti-Submarine Officer on *Laffey*. I learned a lot about electronics, analog computers and acoustic homing torpedoes not to mention bar tending from the customer side of the bar at the Officers Club.

A smarter classmate at my Anti-Submarine Warfare (ASW) school took me to Miami, Florida. We spent several weekends at a motel where the Pan American flight attendants were boarded while in their training. As I recall, the motel was called the Pan Am Airways Motel. I remember waking up on my first Saturday morning there and seeing all those young flight attendant trainees taking the morning sun in their bathing suits around the swimming pool. This Navy life was pretty good so far.

USS *Laffey* was a Sumner class destroyer with about 330 souls aboard including 15 officers almost all of whom were Southerners as was I. One junior officer was from Maine but he seemed to get along well. This was before females were assigned to sea duty. The entire crew was male.

Laffey's primary mission was anti-submarine warfare, and I was the ASW officer. She was an older WWII ship but she had been modernized considerably. She was the second U.S. Navy destroyer to be named *Laffey*. The first Laffey was (DD-459) which was sunk by the Imperial Japanese Navy during the Battle of Guadalcanal in 1942. Both ships were namesakes of a Union sailor who became a hero during the War Between the States.

During WWII, USS *Laffey* (DD-724) achieved a lot of fame as having been the most battle-damaged destroyer to stay afloat after suffering seven direct kamikaze hits and a number of bomb hits in one day. About one third of her crew died in that attack but she amazingly managed to get underway within a couple of days and then limped across the Pacific as a floating wreck to Seattle for repairs. She is now a museum ship moored at Patriots Point near Charleston, SC.

While I served aboard her, she was capable of about 32 knots plus (about 36 mph). That was fairly fast for a ship of that age and time. She was powered by two large steam boilers which fed two 600-pound steam systems. The boilers had super chargers which allowed for sustained high speed operations.

Her main battery of guns consisted of six 5-inch/38 caliber guns in three turrets. Those guns were multi-purpose meaning they could engage surface, air or land targets. As an ensign, I manned one turret of them as a safety observer during general quarters unless we were at Condition 1AS which meant the prosecution of submarines.

Then, I manned and controlled the Underwater Battery Station adjacent to the Combat Information Center just aft of the bridge where the ship was controlled. When prosecuting submarines, I was seated in front of a large analog computer which got direct input from our sonar systems of which we had two. Each cursor my sonarmen placed upon a sonar contact translated into an input into my analog computer. We had a hull-mounted sonar as well as a variable-depth sonar (VDS) which was basically a large fish shaped contraption that was lowered into the water by a sizable winch. It could augment our hull-mounted sonar by getting beneath layer depths of water temperature.

Sound propagation in water has a lot to do with water temperature and changes thereof. A layer of warm water at the top of the water column will trap sonar sound. By putting the VDS below that layer, sonar search range could be increased substantially. We would assess water temperature by periodically dropping bathyther-mograph probes that measured thermal temperatures in the water at various depths as it dropped beneath the ship. That helped us predict sonar detection ranges as well as the depth to best deploy our VDS.

As the ASW officer, I supervised a dozen or so sonarmen and a few torpedo-men who operated and maintained the various equip-ment under my charge. The sonarmen operated and maintained the sonar systems. In effect they were trained to be electronic tech-nicians as well as sonar operators. Sonarmen were screened in part

USS *Laffey* (DD-724)

for their musical ability because they needed a good ear. So, by default I also ended up in charge of the ship's band. I have very little musical ability, but I very much enjoyed finding gigs for the more talented, musical sailors who worked for me.

A particular good memory has to do with *Laffey's* visit to Venice, Italy, where the ship moored in the Grand Canal near St. Mark's Square. A nearby bar was Harry's Bar made famous by Ernest Hemingway whose watering hole it was and who tended to hold forth there. The ship's band set up their equipment on our flight deck and began to play Beatles music including "Ob-la-Di, Ob-la-Da." In no time at all we had a large audience of local Italians and tourists clapping and dancing next to the ship well into the night.

The ship also had an embarked drone anti-submarine helicopter (DASH) that could drop acoustic homing torpedoes on submarine contacts. I was not in charge of the operation or maintenance of that aircraft but we practiced close coordination in a tactical operation sense.

While we were deployed to the Mediterranean, we picked up a sonar contact which we determined to be a nuclear-powered Russian submarine. Using the UQC "underwater telephone," I initiated authentication procedures which involved sending a challenge to the submarine. If the submarine were a U.S. Navy vessel it would respond with a correct coded response. Instead of responding to the challenge, the vessel went to flank speed in order to leave the scene. It made as much noise as a lawn mower which clued us it was Russian. I recorded all our contact with the vessel and later sent the tape to authorities for analysis. The Russian eventually out-ran us at high speed.

As a very junior officer, I wobbled on my new sea-legs at first. I was cognizant of this short coming. I lacked self-confidence but I came up to speed fairly quickly. At first, I stood bridge watches as a Junior Officer of the Deck conning (driving) the ship on an under-instruction basis. Conning a destroyer can be complicated, difficult and nerve wracking. We were typically operating as one of a number of escorts for a carrier battle group. We had to change stations around the carrier on a frequent basis and often under conditions of darkness, low visibility and/or high seas.

Quite often my ship was assigned plane guard duty which meant taking precise station 1,000 yards astern the carrier. As a plane guard we had two basic functions: First, aircraft approaching the carrier for a landing would use us as a reference point for their landing approach. We had to be precise and meticulous in our station keeping. This was particularly important in conditions of reduced visibility (rain, fog or night). Second, we were tasked with trying to rescue air crew survivors if the aircraft crashed against the stern of the carrier or went overboard for some other reason.

Our motor whale boat was always in the boat davits and manned and ready while we were in plane guard position. That happened a couple or three times, once when I was conning the ship. I don't recall ever being able to actually rescue anyone but once we did retrieve a bloody flight helmet.

Soon I gained more confidence in ship handling. Typically, we used grease pencils directly on our surface radar consoles or perhaps pencils on paper maneuvering boards to figure out geometric solutions involving time, distance and speed problems as we maneuvered to change stations or adapt to speed and course changes by the carrier. After a while, I was able to solve those problems in my head. Also, I became adept at the communication skills required in dealing with other ships in company as well as dealing with our propulsion engineering crew well below decks. The Commanding Officer and the Senior Watch Officer had their eyes on me, and they approved me in terms of qualifying me as a full Fleet Officer of the Deck. I was allowed to take full responsibility for the ship operations on my own.

Not long after I qualified as a full Fleet Officer of the Deck, I conned the ship through the Strait of Messina which separates Sicily and Italy. We transited from south to north from the Mediterranean Sea bound for Naples, Italy. We were in company with several destroyers and were steaming in a line-ahead formation with 1,000 yards between us. At first light we approached the sea buoy that marks the start of the Strait. A lot of ship traffic passes through that relatively narrow and restricted area. I estimated at least 30 to 40 other vessels, mostly freighters and tankers, were converging on the same sea buoy at the same time as were we.

I have never trusted commercial ships in situations like that. Commercial ships such as freighters and tankers have fewer or maybe even no lookouts stationed and may in fact be relying on automatic steering controls called Iron Mike. The conning officer might be in the chart house aft of the bridge updating the navigational track of the ship instead of actively managing the movements of the ship. Cruise ships might be better manned and more attentive to control of the ship, but they are often harder to judge at night because of the myriad and confusing lights they show. One can easily misjudge their aspect and therefore their relative movement in conditions of poor light. In other words, I did not necessarily trust the situational awareness of commercial ships.

Due to the confusion of so many ships coming together at one time we had to vary our speed constantly to avoid dangerous situations and to maintain our line-ahead formation. I soon gave up trying to keep more than approximate station relative to the other destroyers sailing in company. That was nerve wracking chaos but afterwards I felt I had experienced a challenge and I had risen to it well.

In condition 1AS or General Quarters for prosecution of submarines, I, as ASW officer, was given control of the ship from my Underwater Battery battle station where I focused on sonar displays of the submarine position. I had to think then in three dimensions as opposed to two. This even though I never had a clear picture of submarine depth except for hints based upon guess work and the bathythermograph profile. Although I was given control of the ship, I could not see what surface ships around us were doing. So, all my maneuvering orders were subject to revision by the General Quarters Officer of the Deck if he felt the ship was in danger of a collision.

Aside from the DASH helicopter, I had control over our deck-mounted shipboard torpedo tubes which were loaded with six modern acoustic homing torpedoes in each set of tubes. More torpedoes were available in a magazine near and on the same deck level as the deck mounted torpedo tubes. Further, the ship had an older antisubmarine mortar system (Hedge Hog) which could launch a circular pattern of rather large explosive mortars at submarine targets ahead of the ship. As I matured in terms of my tactical skills, I learned to aim my torpedoes slightly to the right of a target. The torpedoes were programed to turn to port when searching for a target after an initial run of a thousand yards or so from the ship. The idea was to have the torpedo "wake up" and search at a programmed search point. If I did it right, the first thing the torpedo would see as it "woke up" and turned to port was a submarine target. As ASW officer I also controlled the underwater telephone and could send verbal signals to submarines so as to challenge them in terms of identification and authentication signals

Laffey was a traditional ship. East coast ships tended to be spit and shine and rather rigid in terms of protocol. The bridge watch was typically required to dress in the uniform of the day which was the equivalent of a business suit for all on watch. Officers were likewise required to dress for dinner in the wardroom which usually entailed wearing a tie except when in tropical waters and in white uniforms.

Sometimes, junior officers were required to speak on various subjects after dinner in the wardroom. This was intended to groom our public speaking abilities. We never knew the subject of what we were going to speak on until we looked under our dinner plate. The executive officer would put a slip of paper under the plate of whomever the speaker was to be. That slip of paper might say, "Talk about the role of Italy in NATO" or perhaps "Describe the importance of Lord Nelson in terms of modern naval strategy." I enjoyed those challenges, but many did not.

An important formative and life-long lesson I learned on the *Laffey* was that of taking care of my sailors. I began to realize some of my senior enlisted people were poor people managers and sometimes outrightly prejudiced. So, I stepped up and made it a primary focus particularly with very junior sailors. The groups I had direct responsibility for almost always had the highest reenlistment rates in any command I served under.

I particularly remember a young sailor, assigned to me, who was very much off-balance in the Navy. He came from a small mountain community in North Carolina and he was lost in terms of adapting to the cramped quarters on the *Laffey* and a lack of close friends. I counseled him and came to realize how I might help him adjust. First, I realized he was very connected to his mother but he was not writing to her often enough. So, I ordered him to write to his mother at least once a week and to give me those letters so I could post them. I never opened them or read them but I kept track of his correspondence home. His mother began to write to him more often because she was getting his increased volume of letters. His morale improved right away.

Also, I learned he missed being the audio-visual guy in his church which to him had been a very important distinction. Knowing he had such a talent, I began to tout it among other officers and senior petty officers all of whom needed audio-visual people for the considerable training we conducted on the ship. Suddenly, he gained a sense of importance as well as a bit of swagger. Plus, he picked up new friends around the ship. Soon, he was a much better and more well-adjusted sailor.

Another lesson about taking care of my sailors came about from a rather mundane duty required of junior officers. We had to inspect the meals served to the crew. Typically, the food service was good and many officers were very casual in their inspections. In one of my first inspections, I happened to notice all the salt shakers were clogged.

I decided to make a big deal of that. First, I gave a heads-up to the Supply Officer who was in charge of the crew mess and I then handed my routine inspection report in person to the Executive Officer along with a couple of clogged saltshakers as evidence. I told the Executive Officer my sailors did not like clogged saltshakers but he would never hear from them. That was my job. Miraculously, by the next meal all saltshakers were free flowing and clean. I did not tell the crew anything about this. But sailors are very astute. They notice little things. My stock as someone who cares rose among them.

Another thing I noticed was that the crew did not trust certain officers when they conned the ship. When I was a junior officer of the deck, I observed some sailors sleeping outside on the hard steel weather decks when certain officers had the watch. They feared collisions or other disasters. I vowed to be the best conning officer I could be. I don't recall any crewmen sleeping on the weather decks when I had the Officer of the Deck watch.

I spent a good deal of time at sea on *Laffey*: a six-month Mediterranean cruise plus a three-month cruise to the Caribbean area as well as some weeks of refresher training in and around Guantanamo

Cuba. I was fairly salty when I left her for my next duty assignment. I had visited Lisbon, Portugal; Portsmouth and London, England; Naples, Italy; Malta, Venice, Italy; Athens, Greece; San Juan, Puerto Rico; Christiansted and Frederiksted in the Virgin Islands as well as Guantanamo (Gitmo) Bay, Cuba. Gitmo was not a very pleasant port of call. For example, the ball fields there were adjacent to active mine fields put there to discourage incursions by the Cubans. Lots of abandoned baseballs were evident near the ball fields. Nobody wanted to pursue a foul ball into a mine field.

The *Laffey's* visit to Athens was fortuitous in that it happened to occur during the Greek National Wine Festival which was really a relic of the ancient Rites of Dionysus. Dionysus was the Greek God of the grape harvest and wine making. The annual celebration took place in a large, pleasant forest-like park near Athens. Large barrels of mostly fortified or resinated wine had been placed on the grounds. Each barrel could have easily accommodated a Volkswagen Beetle.

Attendees to the event purchased drinking mugs for a nominal and inexpensive fee at the entrance of the park. They were then free to roam among the wine barrels sampling as much of the contents of each barrel as they wished. As mentioned, most of the wines were resinated meaning it packed the punch of sherry as opposed to common table wine.

U.S. Navy sailors are for the most part not strangers to drinking but they appeared to be out of their league when it came to drinking Greek wine and the even more potent anise-based ouzo. I have never seen so many drunk people in one place at the same time. Many were passed out and sleeping it off in the shade of trees. Most of these people were Greek nationals but a good number were sailors wearing white uniforms.

I by no means got rich as a junior officer. As I recall, my entry level pay in 1968 was a paltry $250 per month. Plus, officers had to pay for their food on the ship. The mess bill was about $60 per month. I could not afford a car until near the end of my tour nor

Me aboard the *Laffey*, off of Cuba, January 1, 1969

could I afford to live ashore. I lived aboard in my rather small state room which I shared with another junior officer who happened to have been a classmate of mine at Miami University. He was the First Lieutenant of the ship meaning he was in charge of all deck operations including our captain's gig as well as our motor whale boat and therefore of all the deck force boatswains' mates.

As mentioned, officers paid for their food on the ship. I served as the officer mess caterer for at least two terms. That meant I was in charge of the menu in the wardroom and therefore managed the budget for what the officers contributed to on a monthly basis. Given we were mostly Southerners, when I was the mess caterer, we ate a lot of grits during our breakfast meals and a lot of fried food at other meals. We also enjoyed a lot of other southern cuisine under my stewardship as mess caterer. I had few complaints.

I was the only bachelor of the 15 officers aboard. Married officers received a modest extra allowance for housing. Still, they lived in what amounted to genteel poverty. During our deployment to the Mediterranean, we had a huge rash of divorces among my married officer colleagues. The Commanding Officer and the Executive Officer did not get divorced right away but they did later. Only one married officer among the more junior officers managed to keep his marriage intact. All the rest divorced sooner or later. Their wives, generally young college graduates, simply could not abide the separations, the lack of adequate income and their rather harsh cultural immersion into Navy life. Those who wanted to start a family decided not to. They were thoroughly thwarted in what they wanted from life.

As a bachelor, I became accustomed to taking the duty assignments from my married colleagues particularly on holidays such as Christmas and Thanksgiving and also on occasions such as the first night in port after extended periods at sea. They were shipmates who needed to be home on such occasions.

I am sure I was more easily able to make a career in the Navy because I did not get married for the first half of my 21 years in the Navy. As a bachelor, I was less encumbered in terms of what I could volunteer for including sea duty or hazardous situations. Furthermore, I was less encumbered financially as I went up in rank. Junior officers don't make a lot of money. A lot of factors go into service as a naval officer. Patriotism is important but I do not put it at the top of the list. It's too vague and general. Instead, I think something called unit integrity is higher on the list. When one is bonded closely to shipmates it directly relates to one's morale, motivation and decisions. Finally, life at sea inclusive of the travel involved is sometimes its own reward. Seeing a beautiful sunset at sea is a dopamine rush.

For long years, I have thought about some strange, interrelated events that occurred when my ship was operating independently within the Bermuda Triangle. The Bermuda Triangle is a mythical and mysterious area in the Caribbean Sea. The triangle is defined by points of Puerto Rico, Bermuda and Miami. Many ships and aircraft have been lost in the triangle. Even Christopher Columbus documented strange phenomena there. At some points magnetic and true north coincide. Other magnetic anomalies are common.

While my ship was there, I happened to be in my sonar control spaces in the evening. We were not at general quarters. I just happened to be there when my sonarmen picked up some very strange sonar contacts. I activated the Mark 1A analog computer I normally manned during general quarters when we were prosecuting submarines. I was amazed to find the sonar contacts moving at insane speeds far beyond what any submerged submarine could attain i.e., above 50 knots which was about the maximum my old computer could measure.

We tracked the sonar contacts for a short time until we lost them. Then the radarmen in the adjacent CIC announced the sudden appearance on our surface radar of several surface contacts moving at high speeds. I left my station to go into the CIC where I observed what they were talking about. I saw their contacts correlated in terms of range and bearing to where our sonar contacts had been lost. Not long after, the surface radar contacts disappeared only to be picked up by our air search radar. In other words, we had detected contacts that went from sub-surface to surface and then higher altitude air contacts. Three separate sensors had picked them up.

This was an entirely odd and unexplained event which still gives me pause even to this day. I wish I had had the presence of mind to use the tape recorder I had at my disposal to record the sonar contacts for further analysis by experts ashore. Unfortunately, I did not have that presence of mind. I have related this story to a number of people who always ask me what it was I thought I saw. I tell them I am agnostic about UFO theories but I still, to this day, wonder. My experience was too compelling to simply file away in my brain as an anomaly.

A KENTUCKY BOY GOES TO SEA AS A NAVAL OFFICER

CHAPTER 4

My Second Ship:
USS *Chowanoc* (ATF-100)

M y two years on my first ship, USS *Laffey*, were successful. I had gained a good regard from my superior officers including my Executive Officer who came to *Laffey* after a tour at the Navy Personnel Bureau in Washington, D.C. He could and in fact did pull some strings in terms of me getting my next job. He was instrumental in obtaining for me the position of Executive Officer (second in command) and Navigator on a smaller ship: USS *Chowanoc* (ATF-100) based out of San Diego. I was quite full of myself for being second in command while I was still a junior officer.

By then, I owned a car. It was a sporty little English Ford which I drove from Norfolk, Virginia, to San Diego, California. That was the first of several times I drove from one coast to another during my career. Typically, it was a six-day trip. When my ship was at sea, I would rent garage space where I would store the vehicle.

The *Chowanoc*, a relic of WWII, was an ocean-going fleet tug and salvage ship, 205 feet long with a draft of 14 feet, with a crew of some 80 sailors (five or so were divers) and six officers. Her only major armament was an old, open 3-inch, .50-caliber slow fire gun. She had a diesel electric power plant and could almost go a quarter-way around the world without refueling but never at high speed. She was extremely powerful in that she could tow heavy ships for long distances but she was not fast. Her rudder was close to the size of a barn door. Without a tow she could do maybe 15 knots. With a tow astern, she could make with luck perhaps five knots. She was named as a tribute to an extinct native American tribe from northeastern North Carolina.

I remember towing a large ship for a long distance in the vast expanses of the Pacific Ocean. The vessel had a large sail area. Some days, depending on wind and current, we covered only about ten miles and some days we lost five miles. That's quite depressing when you have a thousand miles or more to go.

What was my day like as navigator on a U.S. Navy ship? It started very early and ended late. Typically, I was in the chart house just aft of the bridge by 5:00 AM or earlier to review what stars I was going to shoot with a sextant. Most often I relied on the stars Betelgeuse, Rigel and Sirius while in the Pacific Ocean. Those stars were bright and they were about sixty degrees above the horizon which is optimal for navigational purposes. I needed to do this very early in the morning because I needed to be able to see both the stars before they disappeared with a new morning as well as a defined sea horizon that came with a rising sun.

This was antique science devised by early sailors such as Vasco de Gama. Using only my sextant, I would precisely measure the height of the star above the horizon. My quartermaster assistant would write down my observations on the several stars and the exact time they were taken and then we would retire to the chart house to reduce the data to a navigational fix.

In essence, and with reliance on Navy publications like "H.O. 214," we would draw lines between the centers of the stars and the center of the earth. Then we would determine the precise point on the earth those lines intersected the surface of the earth. We would then draw a line of bearing on our chart to that point for each star

USS *Chowanoc* (ATF-100), my second ship

we shot with the sextant. The intersection of those lines of bearing defined where we were at sea. My quarter master assistant said I was a natural with the sextant because I could consistently produce a fix where the several lines of bearing coincided rather exactly. Normally, a celestial fix had an accuracy of five miles or so. Mine were typically much tighter than that. I ascribed it to having very good sight and steady hands.

About ten o'clock in the morning I would shoot the height of the sun. That measurement gave us a "sun line" or measurement of latitude to compare with our earlier celestial fix. Then at about noon I would again shoot the sun with my sextant several times in an effort to determine its zenith or the point at which it ceased to rise and began to fall. That measurement defined "Local Apparent Noon." That was another slightly more accurate measurement that established latitude. Later in the afternoon I would take another sun line. Then towards evening when the stars began to appear and when the horizon was still defined, I would take another celestial star fix.

Every time we established our position by stars or the sun, we would verify our position with LORAN (a long-range navigational system that varied in reliability depending on coverage) or by Satellite which was at that time an emerging technology. We would also take Fathometer readings to measure the ocean depth and compare that to the charts of where we thought we were.

To this day, the Navy relies upon the ancient ways of navigation even though satellite navigation is quicker and easier. That is because we cannot depend on satellites being there after the outbreak of a major war. Satellites will be early casualties of such a war. The stars will still be there.

Challenging to me was the fact, that although I was second in command, I was at only 24 years old, the youngest officer aboard except for the very green supply officer. Command of that kind of ship was the special purview of Limited Duty Officers. Limited Duty officers could not command combatant ships of the line but could command auxiliary ships like ocean-going tugs. Warrant Officers who were generally crusty former enlisted types promoted to officer rank, also tended to serve on this kind of ship as department heads.

During my time aboard *Chowanoc*, I had two commanding officers to whom I was their second in command. Both were very memorable and capable career naval officers. The first was a former Machinist Mate who gained the rank of lieutenant commander and the second was a former quartermaster who also gained the rank of lieutenant commander. The latter was a WWII veteran. He had joined the Navy before I was born. The Chief Engineer of the ship was a Machinist Warrant Officer with about 20 years of service under his belt. The Deck Officer, or First Lieutenant, was a relatively younger but crusty Warrant Bosun. The deck officer was extremely important on a ship such as this in as much as he had direct responsibility for things like towing and salvage operations all of which involved sometimes complex use of our eight-ton boom and other deck equipment. The Operations Officer, also our Diving Officer, was a bit older than I was but I was senior to him. The Supply Officer was a raw ensign who was at sea for the first time.

As mentioned, I initially felt challenged by being second in command of a ship full of officers who were much saltier than I. This was only my second tour at sea. I should not have been so intimidated. All the officers aboard were very kind to me. They faithfully executed all my orders but sometimes they took me aside afterwards and gently counseled me when they thought same to be in the interest of my professional development as well as the interest of the command in general. I listened carefully to their advice and I usually took it. In short order, we arrived at a solid mutual respect.

The culture on *Chowanoc* was very different from that of my first ship, an East Coast spit-and-polish destroyer. My second ship was more like McHale's Navy, much more relaxed but still very professional. The uniform of the day was often swimming trunks. I welcomed this new relaxed culture and maybe I even took it too far when I occasionally walked around the ship with a parrot on my shoulder as if I were a pirate. The crew loved it.

One of the first salvage taskings I experienced while on *Chowanoc* occurred not long after I joined her. A Mexican navy destroyer went aground in Mexican waters in foggy weather conditions not too far south of San Diego near Rosarita Beach. We were ordered to assist the stranded ship and if possible, get her refloated. Upon arrival at the scene, we noticed the stern of the stranded vessel was moving from side to side while the forward section of the ship was stable and not moving at all. We deduced that the keel, or back-bone of the ship, had been broken. The Mexican ship was hard aground. If the keel had not been broken, our correct course of action would have been to maneuver our ship so as to place our stern close to the stricken vessel while meanwhile deploying our two anchors in a hammerlock pattern to seaward. We would then be in a position to pass our towing cable to the stranded ship and be able to use the anchoring power equipment in conjunction with our engines to pull the ship off the beaching point. With a broken keel, the ship would have likely sunk once clear of the ground creating a potential hazard to navigation. Upon reporting this state of affairs to our authorities as well as to Mexican naval authorities, a decision was made from above to cease our efforts. We proceeded back to San Diego. I am unsure of what finally happened to the grounded and ruined Mexican ship.

* * * *

I had a girlfriend in San Diego. One day, my birthday in fact, which is the fifth of May (Cinco de Mayo), we were walking around in Tijuana, Mexico, which is just south of San Diego. I liked being there on my birthday because it seemed so festive. As we walked around town, we found a nondescript and unadvertised shop from wherein a lot of birds were squawking. We entered the shop. A Mexican gentleman asked if we were interested in buying a parrot.

I was aware animals, including parrots, could not be brought directly across the border from Mexico into the U.S.A. without a significant and potentially expensive quarantine process. So, I declined. The shop owner had a solution. He opened the mouth of the Mexican red-headed parrot I was attracted to and poured a shot of tequila down its gullet. The parrot immediately passed out. We put the quiet, comatose bird in my girlfriend's purse and crossed back into California without incident.

I was living on *Chowanoc* at the time and took the parrot to my state room late that evening. The next morning it woke up with a bad hangover. I quickly bought a perch and some food (various seeds and hot peppers) for it. It had a persistent hatred towards me but it nonetheless consented to ride on my shoulder when I walked around the ship. I tried hard to teach it to talk without much success. While doing my paperwork in my stateroom with the bird on its perch next to me, I would endlessly repeat, "I am an eagle!" The parrot ignored me. Then one day he said, "Dinner for the crew!" It had been listening to the ship's announcing system while apparently disdaining to listen to me.

The name of the parrot was "Billie." Many parrots are given sexually ambiguous names because it's hard to tell whether they are male or female based on appearance. It was soon apparent he was a male because he hated my guts but doted on my girlfriend and her two young daughters. He would gently nibble their ear lobes and lovingly stroke their hair. As for relations with me, he preferred hostility. I later received orders to an in-country Vietnam job to which I could not bring Billie. So, I gave it to my girlfriend and her daughters. Parrots live very long lives. It may still be in Southern California nursing an old grudge against me.

* * * *

I will never forget my second commanding officer. He was a very skilled seaman who put immense trust in me. Towards the end of every day at sea, after taking the eight o'clock reports from the department heads, I would take those reports to him in his cabin where we would discuss the operations of the day and the plans for the next. He always had a pitcher of cold martinis prepared for our eight o'clock reports ritual. For many, many years, Navy ships had been dry with no drinking aboard allowed. A Secretary of the Navy named Josephus Daniels had outlawed the alcohol. A cruiser named after him was homeported in San Diego. Many sailors saluted that ship with their middle finger. But this was my captain's ship and his rules applied.

When he went ashore in a port of call, he always presented some sort of challenge for me. My job as his second in command often involved rescuing him from potential trouble of his own making. I clearly remember when the ship was detailed to deliver a large de-activated Navy ship from San Diego to San Francisco. I was the Navigator as well as the Executive Officer. As the Navigator, I was very concerned about the catenary or large underwater loop of the heavy steel cable connected to our tow. While at sea, we allowed the loop of the cable to run deep so as to provide a spring between our ship and the tow in case of heavy seas or wave actions. But as we approached shallower coastal waters as in when we were approaching the Golden Gate Strait toward the Golden Gate Bridge to which the strait led, we had to periodically take in the cable to prevent it from dragging on the bottom, which could potentially damage it.

This was nerve-wracking work for me as the navigator in that I was always trying to calculate the depth of the cable versus the charted depth of the water. I constantly had my eye on the tow while giving directions to the deck crew to gradually take in the towing cable. Suddenly, I noticed the tow was getting farther away from us. The tow cable had become disconnected from the towing bridle and our tow was now free to go aground somewhere near the Golden Gate Bridge where it would become a hazard to navigation!

I immediately alerted the Commanding Officer to this situation. He was quite cool. He ordered the ship to take in our towing cable, come about and sent our motor whale boat to the drifting hulk that had been our tow. Our motor whale boat delivered a messenger line to the tow while we maneuvered close enough to reconnect our tow cable to it. We continued into San Francisco where we handed off the tow to harbor tugs. We proceeded to a pier-side berth and then commenced three or so days of liberty for the crew.

My first impulse had been to communicate our problems to the local Navy port authority, but the Commanding Officer forbade it because he thought it was all under control as indeed it was. Once we were moored, he went ashore and was gone for nearly three days. He was in waterfront honkey-tonk bars the entire time.

I became increasingly worried about the absence of the Commanding Officer as the time for our departure drew near. I was faced with a dilemma: I could get the ship underway on time but without him aboard. I would then have to report his absence. I did not want to go there. I sent out search parties but they were unsuccessful in finding him. Finally, a bit after midnight of the night before we were to depart in the early morning, a messenger from our quarterdeck watch informed me he was aboard. What he did not tell me was that he had brought a woman aboard with him. I went to sleep.

The next morning the Commanding Officer could not be roused by my knocking on the door of his cabin. He was apparently too drunk or too hungover to respond. So, I got the ship underway. About mid-morning, after we had again passed back under the Golden Gate Bridge, we proceeded to sea on a southerly course along the California coast towards San Diego. At this point in time, a rather floozy, bleach-blonde and buxom woman came down from the captain's cabin to the wardroom. She was seeking coffee and perhaps some convivial company.

This was well before women went to sea on Navy ships. We welcomed her aboard, gave her a good breakfast and a couple of cups of strong coffee. Then, I asked our young supply officer to give her a tour of the ship. Meanwhile, I convened a meeting of the officers with the object of determining what to do with her. We quickly arrived at a solution. We would sneak into the port of Long Beach (on the way down the coast towards San Diego) and under the cover of darkness we would put her ashore via our motor whale boat. We all kicked in enough money to cover a bus ticket back to San Francisco as well as incidentals such as a meal or two and taxi fares. She was more than happy with this arrangement and seemed to regard her impromptu short cruise as a lark. She gave all of us wet kisses when she left. As I recall, this was the first but not the last time I got my captain out of trouble. We arrived back in San Diego on time as if nothing had happened.

The ship deployed to the Western Pacific for eight months. An interesting incident happened during our long transit to that theater of operations. As we transited the San Bernardino Strait through the lovely Philippine Islands, a young mess cook went missing one evening. We didn't realize he was missing until he failed to show up at muster the next morning.

The San Bernardino Strait is a sinuous long trek through the myriad islands of the Philippines. As the navigator it was my job to thread our way through it. It included passing through the islands and several inland seas. No sleep for me during the 25 hour sea detail.

When we realized we had a missing crewman we began to try to reconstruct the circumstances of his disappearance. I and others interviewed the petty officer who had been supervising him on the mess deck. That petty officer told us the mess cook had been detailed to throw bags of garbage over the fantail after the evening meal for the crew. We quickly deduced he must have fallen overboard while doing so.

Next, we tried to nail down the time when he might have been dumping the garbage. I instructed my leading quartermaster, my main navigation assistant, to break out the special charts that predicted currents in that specific area where we thought he must have fallen overboard. Resorting to time and distance calculations, we arrived at a predicted point where he might be, given that he had fallen overboard more than twelve hours ago. We turned around and proceeded to that point. We were right on in our calculations.

We found him precisely where our calculations predicted he would be. Luckily, the sailor, who was not wearing a life jacket, had clung to a plastic garbage bag and had in fact undone the bag in order to blow more air into it so as to make it more buoyant. He was exceedingly glad to see us when we found him. He had been very lucky on at least a couple of counts. First, the wind and weather had been calm allowing my navigation team to better trust the current charts that led us to him. Secondly, sharks would often follow ships such as ours seeking the garbage we threw overboard. He had no troubles with sharks.

I sometimes wonder if that young sailor ever re-enlisted. I never knew because I was transferred off the ship when it came time for him to make that decision. Imagine what he went through that long sleepless and scary star-lit night clinging to his garbage bag. He likely knew nobody had seen him go overboard. He probably thought he had no hope of being rescued. I wager he probably decided that night he had had enough of the Navy.

Much of the time after arriving at our theater of operations we spent in and around Vietnam performing towing and salvage missions. One of those missions had us delivering a section of floating dry dock into the port of Vung Tau. As I recall, we picked that vessel up in Singapore.

We had the bad luck to encounter a strong typhoon at sea. In the Pacific, there are no hurricanes. They are known as typhoons. I am lucky to have never been prone to sea sickness but everyone else aboard seemed to be very sick. The section of drydock had a large sail area. At times it towed the ship as opposed to the ship towing it. We constantly changed our movement reports as we struggled with the typhoon. For maybe that reason the Fleet Weather Center in Guam lost track of us.

We reported very grim weather with 90 mile an hour winds that were literally blowing the paint and antennas off of the ship. Huge waves would develop only to be cut down by the high winds that howled loudly and constantly. We thought we might have to cut our tow loose but it did somewhat stabilize the ship even though it towed us backward.

Weather like that is exhausting to the ship's company. Sleep was impossible and everyone had to strap themselves into their bunks to avoid being tossed out of their bunks. Furthermore, eating was practically impossible except for crackers and such. Even the simplest of chores was exhausting. The passageways in the ship sloshed with sea water and vomit.

We began to worry our main diesel-electric motor might take on water and short out. That would have been catastrophic because we would lose propulsion and in turn the ship could seek the troughs of the seas and possibly turn over and sink. Suddenly, nobody was seasick. I then learned fear cancels sea sickness.

Finally, the Fleet Weather Center in Guam managed to get a handle on our position and warned us we were in the un-navigable semi-circle of the typhoon and therefore in danger. We took appropriate action to get into the navigable semi-circle and gradually the weather began to ease. After enduring some more very high seas and contrary winds we pulled into the outer harbor of Vung Tau where we handed our tow off to local U.S. Navy harbor tugs.

The plan was to then go back to sea but the Captain decided he was thirsty and wished to wet his whistle ashore. So, he turned to me as the navigator and told me to chart a course into the inner harbor where we could tie up at a pier. After a brief consultation with the local charts and the tide tables I informed the Captain the tide was going out and we could not hope to get over a shallow sand bar that separated the outer harbor from the inner. I also reminded him we had no diplomatic clearance to pull into the port nor did we have any funny money (military script) to spend there. He reminded me of his thirst and reemphasized to me his desire to go in.

One way to end a Navy career is to put a ship aground and I was about to do that. We proceeded towards the inner harbor at slow speed. We hit the sand bar. The ship listed to port in a sickening way. I ordered back full but the Captain countermanded my order and ordered full speed ahead. I briefly considered ordering the quarter master of the watch to enter all this into the log as a personal protection but I didn't. I was too loyal to the Captain to do so.

The ship stuttered and then came to a full stop. Then it acted like a dog humping a leg for a minute or two. Then, *spoit* as it cleared the sand bar and we went into the deeper inner harbor. We tied up to a pier and the Captain went ashore where he hooked up for the evening with U.S. Navy types who had a drinking establishment of some sort there.

The Captain was the only one to go ashore. I ordered the crew to stay aboard and I sent divers down to inspect our hull for damage. The divers reported no damage beyond a lot of scrapped off paint under the hull. Late that dark evening, a mike boat (a medium sized amphibious landing craft) tied up to our ship. The coxswain of the boat announced our Captain had traded everything in his boat for four cases of steaks from our shipboard freezer.

I ordered the duty officer to assemble a work party to break out four cases of steaks, put them in the boat and off-load everything in it onto the ship. It was dark and I could not clearly see what was in the boat. It turned out to be a good number of cases of beer, about 90 rounds of light anti-tank weapons (LAWS) (collapsible bazooka-like weapons firing 2.5-inch rockets) and a young puppy.

The puppy, whom the crew christened "Mary" in honor of the rather homely spouse of the Chief Boatswain Mate became everyone's personal pet and a wonderful ship's mascot. The corpsman established a health record for her and by some means ministered to her needed rabies and distemper vaccinations. The boatswain's mates fashioned for her a small personal life vest. The personnel clerk maintained a service file for her documenting service ribbons, advancements in rank, etc. At sea, Mary stood watch in the pilot house and in port she was always with the quarter-deck watch near the gang plank. She gravitated to where most of her sailors were. At mealtimes she went to the mess decks where she was well fed and lavished with a lot of attention by the crew. Mary became a good shipmate to all as well as a crew member dedicated to her ship. She barked at harbor tugs and seemed to consider them to be lesser entities.

Early the next morning, the U.S. Navy authorities in Vung Tau warned us that the Viet Cong had put up rocket aiming stakes in the shallows near our ship during the night. These were preparatory to conducting a rocket attack against our ship. We quickly prepared to get under way. The tide was right for getting over the sand bar and we went to sea without incident.

It was a Sunday morning when we were back at sea. The Captain decided we should have a holiday barbeque on the fan tail. We used cut-in-half 50-gallon drums as barbeque pits. He also decreed every crewman could have a few beers to wash down the barbeque.

He further specified each crewman could shoot two or three of the LAWS weapons for their amusement. The sailors took to throwing steak scraps over the fantail, guzzling beer and then shooting at the sea gulls with the LAWS. The LAWS produced tremendously loud explosions when they hit something.

Everyone was enjoying all this until two beer-drinking sailors got into a fight. One cut the other with a rather superficial knife slash to the belly of the other. I was worried about the potential legal ramifications: sailors drinking beer at sea, cutting one another with knives and shooting LAWS for amusement. I expressed my concerns to the Captain who shrugged them off. He brought the two offending sailors together with me in his cabin. He got the two sailors to shake hands and swear not to hurt one another again. Problem solved. No legal issues. Elegant and simple.

I was not a trained navy diver but we had several crewmen aboard who were professional divers. When the ship called at Guam for a visit, I learned that one of our divers had at some time previously dived into a fresh water filled cave in Guam. The divers were considering a dive into that body of fresh water that communicated with the ocean. In essence, it was an underground cave and river going into the ocean. The Japanese had used this underground river of sorts as a source of fresh water during WWII when they occupied the island.

I asked the divers to take me along on their exploration of this interesting place. At first, they were reluctant to do so but I pressed my case. After all, I was senior to all of them. They required me to undergo some basic scuba diving training before they would agree to take me along. Finally, they relented and off we went. Our total number was probably four or five people.

We arrived at what looked like a small sized pond where we put on our equipment including rubber diving suits, scuba tanks, flashlights, etc. Then I entered the water with qualified divers ahead of and behind me to watch over me. Shortly after we descended into the cave system, we came upon piping, tools and other implements left behind by the

Japanese a good many years ago when WWII was raging. As we descended further into the cave system, which at points was restricted, it became dark and we had to rely on flashlights to guide our progress. I confess to feeling a bit of claustrophobia and trepidation about what would happen to us if we had a problem with our diving equipment. But perhaps less than an hour into the venture, we saw dim sunlight ahead of us.

We had reached the ocean via the cave system. I was not sure where we went from fresh water to salt water. Our motor whale boat was waiting to pick us up thanks to the advanced study and planning of our divers. I enjoyed this illicit jaunt immensely and I thanked the divers who bent the rules in taking me.

The *Chowanoc* fairly frequently called at ports in Taiwan (also known as Formosa in Portuguese). The most frequent ports we visited were Keelung or Kao-Hsiung on the western coastline where most of the best harbors are located. Occasionally we would foray via land to the capital city of Taipei. Sometimes we were tasked to serve as a mooring platform for older diesel-electric submarines patrolling the Taiwan Strait between Taiwan and mainland China. The U.S. Navy patrolled the Strait on a routine basis because China has long claimed and threatened Taiwan.

The diesel-electric submarines were referred to as "pig boats" for good reason. For one thing the boats were small and cramped. The crew hot-bunked because there were not enough bunks aboard for everyone to go to bed at once. Hot bunking means a sailor would find an empty bunk and put his personal "fart sack" in it and then sleep in it until had to find another bunk. During their patrols, they were not allowed to dump trash or garbage while on patrol so as to avoid giving away their location. Instead of dumping the trash and garbage, they stored it aboard in the shower stalls, clothes washing machines and dryers where it tended to rather quickly rot and become noxious.

When we were serving as a mooring platform we would typically anchor and the submarine would tie up to our ship. Upon opening the hatches, a slightly green colored gas would come up from the submarine. The gas was that coming from the rotting garbage and trash aboard. The crew and officers looked somewhat disheveled. Most were bearded because they did not tend to shave or for that matter bathe while at sea. Most had ugly and old sweat stains around their arm pits.

We would have a vehicle or two, including our motor whale boat, ready to take the crew ashore where they would bathe and otherwise clean up in what were called "hotsey baths." We also provided the people who would serve as duty drivers for them. Being a duty driver was not a desired assignment in that circumstance. The crewmen that were detailed to perform this duty would complain about the smell they endured from the submarine sailors who were their passengers.

Ships deployed to the Western Pacific typically visited a number of ports in Japan, Thailand, South Korea, Singapore, etc. The most popular with the crew were Hong Kong, China and Subic Bay in the Philippines. Both of the latter ports of call had a lot of sailor bars among other amenities of various types attractive to sailors.

In Subic bay, the town of Olongapo had more bars than any other kinds of enterprises. Most were stacked up on multiple floors in the center of town. I hated it when I drew shore patrol duty there. I knew I was in for a long night of bloody brawls and drunken sailors.

What I remember very fondly was getting a haircut in the Philippines. The barbershops were open-air affairs situated in the shade of a tree. The client would take a chair and several things would happen at the same time. A young girl would take off your shoes and would polish them until they gleamed. Another girl would put a cold San Miguel beer in your hand and the barber would provide some kind of clay based facial and a relaxing haircut. All for about a dollar. If the client had a hangover it would be gone by the end of the therapeutic experience.

My favorite port of call in the Pacific was that of Hong Kong. The food, drink and ambiance were exceptional. The floating restaurants were particularly memorable. Upon pulling into port, a Chinese woman named Mary Sue would board the ship. Mary Sue ran a sizable orphanage in Hong Kong. She would negotiate with the leading boatswain mate. The deal was always the same. She would want permission to set up a soft drink concession and to sell cold soft drink beverages to the crew for as long as the ship was in port. Then the boatswain would offer all of the brass he had scrounged up long before the deployment. That was usually in the form of expended shell casings and perhaps other brass items he had been gathering long before the ship left the States. Sometimes the boatswain offered to trade used mooring lines. If the offer was at all substantial, Mary Sue's orphans would paint the entire ship with rags and paint provided by the ship. When the ship left port, it would be gleaming. The crew would be happy because they did not have to do any work painting the ship while in port.

I remember the many tailors for which Hong Kong was well known. They did a fine, on-time, minimal cost job when it came to providing me with high quality new suits, uniforms and even tailor-made shoes often under short time constraints.

On a side-note: during my tour as Executive Officer on *Chowanoc* I was assisted by a wonderful multi-talented sailor whose name was Richard Harrison. You may recall him as the "Old Man" on the famous reality TV show known as *Pawn Stars*. At the time we were serving together, I knew him as Personnel Man First Class Harrison. His nominal job was that of maintaining all personnel records on the ship. But he also ran the ship post office and he functioned as our disbursing officer in charge of all pay functions for the crew and officers aboard. He was of inestimable help to me in terms of shipboard administration. After he retired from the Navy, he and his wife ventured into real estate in the Los Angeles area. That did not work out as well as he had hoped. He opened a pawn shop in Las Vegas and the rest is history. His reality TV show took off big time.

I kept in touch with him. Some years later after I retired, I was in Las Vegas with some old Navy friends and I looked him up. He graciously invited a friend and me to lunch and then back to his pawn shop where he happened to be filming an episode of his show. On an impromptu basis he put me into this episode which drew on his Navy experiences.

Another interesting but disastrous incident happened toward the end of my tour on *Chowanoc*. We were ordered to assist in conducting shock or explosive blast tests on an old decommissioned cruiser. We towed the large cruiser to the Los Coronado Islands off the coast of southern California and moored her to some very large concrete clumps we put in place on the deep ocean bottom. The object of the tests was to position the cruiser and then set off increasingly larger explosive charges at increasingly closer ranges to the ship which had been fitted with a variety of seismic devices to record the effect of the detonations. The detonations were so calculated to simulate nuclear explosions at various ranges. The tests were conducted over a several-day period.

We were assisted by people and a boat from an amphibious command based near San Diego. A naval architect did much of the planning and guidance in terms of how big the explosive charges were to be and at what ranges from the cruiser they were to be detonated. A specially configured mike boat (utility boat) streamed the charges with steel cables from a large winch welded to the deck of the mike boat. The naval architect controlled the positioning and detonation of the charges. Then, our boat would transfer people to the cruiser to make note of the readings on the seismic devices placed beforehand on the ship.

The detonations killed a lot of fish which in turn provoked a lot of excited feeding frenzies by the considerable number of great white sharks around the Los Coronado Islands. The last explosive charge was the largest of all and the closest to the cruiser. It was almost under the cruiser. When it went off, the cruiser came out of the water, broke in half and then rather quickly sank. It was quite a sight to see but everyone's attention was instead riveted by the disaster taking place on the mike boat.

The last and final explosion caused the cable being streamed from the mike boat to whip lash in severe fashion. The large winch from which it was being streamed broke from the welds securing it to the deck. The first of five sailors to die in very quick order in this disaster was a Combat Camera crewman detailed to film the test. He had taken position just aft of the winch. When it broke loose, it snarled like a huge bird nest then went overboard carrying the photographer to the bottom with it. We recovered his movie camera from the deck but we were unable to retrieve the body of the photographer. Apparently, he became entangled in the bird nest that was the snarled winch cables. The winch in turn got tangled up in the very heavy concrete clumps we had placed to moor the cruiser. Later, we tried to raise the winch with the eight-ton boom of the *Chowanoc* but to no avail. It would not budge.

The failure of the winch also knocked overboard four other sailors from the mike boat. *Chowanoc* had a semi-rigid inflatable Zodiac type safety boat in the water manned with a coxswain and a couple of our divers wearing wet suits. We ordered them to assist in rescuing the sailors who had been knocked overboard. We received a very disturbing response via radio from the safety boat to somewhat this effect: "Sir, we are unable to comply. Sharks are bumping our boat trying to get at us. We can't get in the water."

The safety boat did try to get one of the sailors into the safety boat but that sailor in the water insisted the boat immediately proceed to another sailor who appeared to be seriously injured. They could not find neither the sailor who was reportedly injured nor could they find the first sailor when they came back to get him. Sharks apparently pulled both down. The safety boat did manage to pull one sailor aboard and they delivered him aboard *Chowanoc* in short order. He was missing a leg above his knee and he was in shock. In spite of the best emergency efforts of our corpsman, he quickly bled out and died on our main deck. He was a first-class yeoman scheduled to retire within a week.

My Commanding Officer was deeply involved with trying to

deal with this emergency on the functional level of handling the ship and dealing with what needed to be done now. So, I decided my best efforts would be devoted to communicating with our superior officer who was a Navy captain acting on behalf of the Navy Service Squadron (based in San Diego) to which we reported.

I sent an urgent short message to him communicating the basics of our situation. I included the news we had lost five sailors. That was technically correct but it was not good reporting, I was shaken by what I had just seen and experienced. I learned something important that day: wait a bit and gather my wits before sending communications like that. Accuracy is way more important than urgency unless you need immediate assistance. The Service Squadron Command assumed we had lost five crewmen from *Chowanoc* and therefore their larger command: not so. They were all from the assisting amphibious command. That was a very important detail from the perspective of our immediate commander. I cleared that up very quickly in my subsequent communications but I felt like I had not done as well as I could have. Nevertheless, I was not brought to task for my less than perfect performance. I was forgiven.

Later, as Navigator, I regarded the dead photographer as a burial at sea situation. I had previous experience in that regard. I drew up a neat and accurate nautical chart detailing exactly where his body was interred in the ocean. I sent it to his family.

We were accustomed to burials at sea. The Navy decedent affairs office in Washington periodically sent us shoe box sized containers of urns with the cremated ashes of career sailors and officers inside. The Navy has a policy of offering free burials at sea to families of deceased career service members. I would store the ashes in a drawer under my bunk in my stateroom until such time as we could schedule the funeral services. I would tell the commanding officer something like, "I have two lieutenant commanders and a warrant officer under my bunk. We need to bury them." We conducted dignified ceremonies with a firing squad of sailors dressed in full-service uniforms to render gun salutes. I usually oversaw the ceremonies and scattered the ashes myself. I quickly learned the hard way to make sure the wind was blowing in the correct direction before releasing the ashes from the urns. Then I would prepare nautical charts documenting when and where the ashes were interred and send the charts to a designated next of kin.

* * * *

While on *Chowanoc*, I had a brief but very pleasurable affair with a young Japanese woman while my ship was visiting Sasebo. I met her in a stand bar located in a mall-like setting. A stand bar is a small bar with maybe five bar stools. She was tending the bar. Neither of us spoke one another's language beyond yes and no but that was sufficient for our rather short time together. It was a passionate relationship reduced to the basics of yes and no.

I walked into her bar with several bags of art supplies purchased from a nearby art store. I have always been an amateur but enthusiastic artist. Art supplies at that time were much cheaper in Japan so I loaded up. I remember walking out of that family-run store only to be delayed slightly by the various family members lining up to thank me for my business. I was impressed by their obvious service ethic.

I got as far as the small stand bar where I sat down and apparently impressed Mesune. That's what she told me her name was. Later, I learned that *mesune* means girl in Japanese. I did not know that at the time. I never knew her real name but we got along together very well from the feverish start. Later, she even introduced me to her father which was kind of awkward. He was a Japanese WWII veteran who did not very much like Americans. My father was also a WWII veteran who had spent some five years trying to kill Japanese.

The Commanding Officer of the *Chowanoc* and I maintained friendly contact for years after my tour on *Chowanoc*. We got together once for lunch with our spouses after he retired to a double-wide trailer in Southern Virginia. I was passing through that area at the time. I had by then been promoted to the rank of commander. He expressed dismay at the fact I was not an admiral. I think he was remembering how I saved his ass so many times. He felt the Navy should have better rewarded those efforts which were very laudable to him.

Sadly, he passed away a few years ago. His spouse contacted me and reported he had been diagnosed with fatal symptoms consistent with exposure to Agent Orange. She went on to say the Navy was denying her certain benefits because his exposure to Agent Orange was not reliably documented. Relying on my memory and a cruise book documenting in detail where we were operating in Vietnam, I sent her a carefully crafted letter about when and where he was likely exposed to agent Orange. She successfully used the letter to break the bureaucratic impasse. I felt good about her getting the full benefits she was seeking.

* * * *

Another memory has to do with the Quartermaster First Class who served under me as the Assistant Navigator. He was a model sailor who could have been featured on a recruiting poster. We got along very well together. Among other things, he worked out our celestial star sightings in advance of our morning and evening star fixes. Early one morning, I arrived at the chart house only to find my assistant had overslept. So, I proceeded without him to calculate which stars I was going to sight.

I was chewing tobacco as was my want in those days. I needed to spit. In the chart house I spied an empty Coca Cola bottle which would serve well as a receptacle for my tobacco juice. The quartermaster was somewhat addicted to Coca Cola. He finally woke up and appeared in the chart house while I was on the wing of the bridge. He saw the coke bottle I had been spitting into. He took a big gulp of what he assumed was Coca Cola but what was in fact my tobacco juice.

He angrily accosted me on the bridge wing. He seemed ready to slug me so I rather delicately reminded him I was an officer and sailors are not allowed to slug officers. He restrained himself. And I quit chewing tobacco.

CHAPTER 5

On the Way to My In-country Vietnam Tour

After my time on *Chowanoc*, I had enough time in service to leave the Navy. Unlike enlisted people, regular officers do not re-enlist. Unless they resign, they continue on active duty. I decided the Navy had been good to me thus far. I was also feeling adventurous. I feared boredom.

So, I volunteered for an in-country Vietnam job in 1971. Specifically, I wanted to be a naval advisor to the South Vietnamese pro-western government. It sounded like a worthwhile experience, and maybe it would advance my navy career in a different direction. American advisors worked with the armed forces of the Republic of Vietnam. JFK authorized special forces troops and military advisors in South Vietnam in the early 1960s. There were 16,000 military advisors in Vietnam in the mid 1960s, but political corruption and failure of the advisors to understand the culture and language of the Vietnamese led to failure of some of the advisory efforts. I came to regret my decision to volunteer to go in-country to Vietnam but that's for later in this story.

My request was approved. I was then sent to the Defense Language Institute in Monterey, California, for eight pleasant months of Vietnamese language training and chasing women in my spare time. The language training was work but offered plenty of free time, and I was 25. Monterey, California, is a pastoral paradise with dazzling beaches, an ocean rich in wildlife, plus amazing sunsets off the Pacific.

After completing language training, I attended Survival Evasion Resistance and Escape (SERE) training, which took place mostly at a camp near Warner Springs in the southern California mountains. The SERE program was designed to prepare U.S. military personnel, like military advisors in Vietnam, to survive in various situations, including being captured. Between 1959 to 1975, SERE was taught to those at risk of capture and exploitation.

SERE training was arduous. We knew the primary intent of the training was to prepare people going to Vietnam for the potentiality of being captured. My SERE class comprised about eighty trainees, a mix of a few officers, and mostly enlisted sailors. It started with a couple of days of beach survival training on Coronado Island across the bay from San Diego before moving on to Warner Springs.

On Coronado Island, we were issued a small section of a parachute, which we used mostly for shelter, and K-bar fighting knives for use as all-around tools. We were not issued any rations during our SERE training. We were allowed to eat whatever we could catch or gather from the ocean or the mountains which was meager indeed. My fishing and hunting experiences as a young boy turned out to be helpful.

We improvised some crab traps using our parachute scraps while on the beach and managed to dig up some clams. We dug a hole in the sand in which we built a fire and heaped on some seaweed and then steamed our miserable catch. While on the beach, we ate no more than a small mouthful or two. This starvation was intentional preparation for the next phase in the mountains near Warner Springs. We were supposed to be starved and off-balance for that.

At Warner Springs, we had almost nothing to eat, although I do recall we managed to gather a few handfuls of small wild potatoes which did not do more than somewhat flavor a pot of boiling water shared by about 80 people. The training area had been scoured by the many trainees who preceded us. I remember having heard prickly pear cactus were edible, I found one and tried it. The trouble was that one needs to cut off the spines before eating it. I did not know that and suffered for some days with cactus spines in my tongue. Tweezers helped remove the more prominent spines.

According to folklore, a previous class had managed to kill a deer. Legend has it that a young sailor climbed a tree and waited. Against all odds, a deer happened to walk under the tree. The sailor jumped out of the tree and onto the deer which he stabbed with his dull K-bar fighting knife. He then held onto the deer and screamed until his hungry classmates came to his assistance and proceeded to kick the deer to death. I am not so sure this really happened but it is nonetheless a good story.

Upon arrival at Warner Springs, we received some very cursory training in land navigation. Then we were given a destination to walk to with the promise of an orange if we got there. As I recall, only two or three, out of eighty or so trainees managed to get to the destination point. The rest of us were captured before getting there. Our "hostile" opponents set up machine guns which were firing blanks, but we did not know they were blanks. The guns were located at predictable points usually at crossings on dirt roads where the enemy could easily swoop in to capture us.

Upon being herded into our prison camp the fun and games commenced. Many of us were water-boarded to the point of passing out and/or physically beaten. In my case, I was interrogated and I tried to stick to Geneva Convention Standards in terms of name, rank and serial number. I was immediately subjected to the water board. I was strapped to a board with my feet a good bit higher than my head. A team of torturers poured water down my nose and throat and when I was choking a wet rag was forced into my mouth. I passed out briefly.

What I did not know at the time was some my torturers were

well trained Navy corpsmen. I thought one of them was trying to strangle me but he was really checking my neck for my blood pressure, pulse and general vital signs as I was being tortured.

My interrogation continued. I was asked what my Navy specialization was. Not wanting to be water boarded again, I replied deviously that I did "lots of things." After a few more questions, they beat me up a bit but did not subject me to the water board again. That was a teaching point in the training. You can't stand up to torture so adapt to avoid it.

I was already aware I was the second senior officer in our group. Once in the prison camp, I tried to determine where the senior officer might be. One of the guards made a point of showing me where he was. He was locked down in a semi-flooded hole in the ground less than the size of a dog-house. A pallet was secured with a steel cable over him and that's where he was kept for almost the entire span of that phase of training.

The guard told me I was now the ranking officer. He handcuffed me to a very junior sailor who he identified as "the War Baby." The War Baby was to be a whipping boy. Any time I made the guards mad, which was constantly, they beat him up or subjected us both to very cold water hosing at night in the frigid weather of the mountains.

I had a fairly trim physique at the time. After enduring those frequent cold water hosing downs in the nude at night in the mountains I began to recall Michelangelo's sculpture of David. I always wondered why David's penis was so small. Now I understood. He must have been as cold, wet and exhausted as I was at the time.

After about two days of enduring his lot as the War Baby, the young sailor showed definite signs of mental distress. The guards fired him and assigned another young sailor to take over as the War Baby. They picked a baby-faced, slim sailor but they picked the wrong guy. He was a junior SEAL team member who was tough as nails. I can remember a guard picking him up by his ankles and then beating his body on the ground. The new War

Baby would get up, straighten his uniform, dust himself off, salute me and smile. The guards seemed to go nuts but I could tell they were secretly hiding their admiration for him.

One night, the guards released me from the handcuffs to the War Baby and took me into an underground dirt floored bunker where there were some bunk beds with nobody in the bare metal bedding frames. A small fire in a corner made the place warm. I was given a small platter of warm rice to eat. No demands were made of me. I was exhausted and quickly fell deeply asleep.

During the night, my fellow trainees were paraded by me sleeping in my bunker and the empty rice platter. The guards told them I had agreed to join them in their revolutionary struggle and I was therefore being rewarded.

The next morning, I was given a copy of Mao Tse Tung's *Little Red Book* and was told to read passages from it to my colleagues as they worked. I was further told if I did a good job of that task, they would go easier on the other prisoners and even feed them.

So, I walked among them, as they raked the prison yard with their fingers, reading from the little book. My off-balanced colleagues were hostile to me and would have killed me if they could. When I could do so without being overheard by the guards, I would try to explain to my colleagues that this was all bullshit and tell them how I and they were being set up.

Not long afterwards, I was blindfolded and my hands were tied behind me. I was led to the Commandant's office for more interrogation. I was made to sit on the porch outside his office to await my interview. I suspected I was alone. I got out of my hand bindings and then pulled down my blindfold slightly and saw that I was indeed alone. That took a bit of gumption on my part because they would have subjected me to more water boarding or beaten me for peeking out from my blindfold. I ran from the porch and managed to get out of the compound. I had escaped! I was rather quickly recaptured but my reward was the best tasting and juiciest orange I have ever eaten.

The next morning while we were formed up in the prison yard, the Viet Cong flag was lowered from the flag pole and an American flag was raised. SERE training was over. We were critiqued on our individual performance. I was surprised at the detailed notes our guards had taken on each of us. I later heard one of us, a mid-grade officer, had buckled so badly that his orders to Vietnam had been cancelled. His navy career was over.

Utterly exhausted, I went back to my bachelor officer quarters (BOQ) room in San Diego after a long bus ride. I had not bathed for well more than a week, except for being hosed down from time to time by the guards, in the cold evenings, nor had I eaten much of anything. I poured a hot bath and fell asleep in it. I woke up when the water became cold. I was shivering violently.

I thought about what I had just gone through. I congratulated myself for having gotten through it. I had some doubts about this assignment I was embarking upon. In 1976 there were investigations into SERE training based on reports of abuse. In 1984, SERE training was only given to service men whose position, rank, or seniority made them vulnerable to exploitation. It wasn't until 2018 that waterboarding was banned from training programs.

CHAPTER 6

In-country Vietnam

In late 1971, I boarded a TWA commercial airliner contracted to the military. It took off from McChord Air Force Base in Washington state and was jam-packed with soldiers, sailors and airmen. The trip to Saigon was about twenty hours in duration. We had a refueling stopover at an airbase in Alaska.

We were all wearing light, short-sleeved tropical uniforms in as much as we were headed to Vietnam. Upon landing in Alaska in the darkness, we had to disembark our aircraft per protocol while it was being refueled. It was winter in Alaska. We were told to walk or run to a building a fair distance from our aircraft. We were told hot coffee was available there. I remember the utter sub-zero cold I felt upon getting out of the aircraft. I paused and spit into the air. My spittle immediately froze and it cracked in mid-air before hitting the tarmac as a small piece of ice. We ran to the building in search of hot coffee. Unfortunately, the coffee machine had an "out of order" sign taped to it. Then we repeated in reverse order the process of running to the aircraft to re-board. Many hours later we landed at Tan Son Nhut Air Base outside Saigon. When the doors to the aircraft were opened, a blast of stifling, moist tropical heat instantly filled the aircraft.

The long trip had utterly exhausted everyone aboard the aircraft. Mercifully, we were not expected to be functional for about 48 hours given the time change, the length of our flight and the seasonal stresses we had endured. I checked into an Army BOQ in Saigon and slept like a baby before seeking out the Navy office in Saigon that would process me and help guide me further.

I spent a couple of days in Saigon where I attended some briefings and explored the local restaurants and watering holes. While running around Saigon at night, I happened to come across an old friend from my days at Miami University. He was Major Rich Higgins of the U.S. Marine Corps. He had been a NESEP, or Naval Enlisted Scientific Education Program, student when I was a midshipman at Miami University. Rich was a Kentucky boy like me. He was a couple of years senior to me. We had ride-shared once on a trip to Kentucky during the Christmas holidays. We spent a pleasant evening in a Saigon restaurant catching up. I never saw him again. Some years later, after the war, when Rich was serving on a U.N. peace keeping mission in Lebanon, he was abducted by Hezbollah terrorists and eventually videotaped as he was hanged to his death from a ceiling with a thin wire.

Then, a long jeep ride took me to my new duty station in Nam Can, an unpleasant but fairly secure floating mobile base camp near the tip of the Mekong Delta. It was called SEA FLOAT. Admiral Zumwalt, Commander, Naval Forces (COMNAVFOR) Vietnam, ordered it to be built with barges. It had a number of "Sea Hut" buildings installed on the barges. It bristled with installed mortars and automatic weapons. The river current was more than six knots, constituting a good defense against Viet Cong swimmers/sappers. Prior to construction, the surrounding area was very much controlled by the Viet Cong. The base had functioned as an important U.S. Navy base and presence on the Mekong Delta area but when I got there about the only U.S. Navy presence consisted of naval advisors and our support personnel.

On the way there, I picked up an M1 Carbine rifle which was my

Sea Float mobile base camp

preferred weapon during my time in Vietnam. It was an old WWII model weapon chambered for 7.62 x 55mm NATO rounds. I loved it. It was lighter, more reliable and easier to deal with than an M16. It was a perfect weapon to throw in the seat of a jeep or into a boat. Importantly, it had a fully automatic fire feature which meant it functioned as a mini-machine gun. I always had two large banana clips duct-taped together to feed it.

I was assigned to a squadron of mixed vessels of the South Vietnamese Navy: armed junks, various sizes of old U.S. Navy amphibious craft, a few minesweeping boats and fast riverine patrol boats. These vessels patrolled the Mekong river as well as the coastal waters near the Mekong Delta. The patrol activities along the coast as well as the river waters were designed to deny the enemy the waterborne logistic routes along the coast and via the Mekong river estuaries. The activities along the coast were carried out by a task force known as Operation Market Time while the activities on the estuary river systems were grouped as a task force called Operation Game Warden. Both task forces were successful in that they forced the enemy to rely on the much more difficult overland Ho Chi Minh Trail for logistic support.

In theory, my tasking was that of an advisor. Quickly, I realized my real job was that of making sure the South Vietnamese naval forces completed their assigned missions. This was my first exposure to the rampant corruption that was the reality in Vietnam. I quickly realized if I did not accompany them on patrols their natural inclinations would lead them to moor in safe places where they could sell ammunition, radios and other such things to the enemy. Then they would report fictitious engagements with Charlie.

The USN officer I was supposed to replace was not there. I was told he had been killed two weeks earlier. I was assigned sleeping quarters in the same metal hut my dead predecessor had occupied. Not having a proper turnover with the U.S. Navy officer who went before me, I was very much on my own. A South Vietnamese navy officer was my counterpart contact and equal in rank to me. I tried to establish a relationship with him but that did not go so well at first. We exchanged pleasantries and introductions upon our first meeting which seemed to go well. I was interested in knowing if he was a Catholic or Buddhist. Most officers in the South Vietnam Navy were Catholic. I wanted to know what he was. Perhaps too soon into our initial meeting I obliquely (I thought) asked him what church he attended.

The Vietnamese language relies upon five linguistic tones. If one butchers the tones it can and most often will distort the meaning of the word one meant to convey. Instead of asking him what house of worship he attended I ended up asking him what house of prostitution he frequented. He clammed up at that point probably thinking it was a very inappropriate question. I had no idea what I had done wrong but I walked away thinking something had gone badly in that meeting. Some days later when I was again talking to him, he said, "Oh, is that what you were asking me?" Both of us were amused once we realized my gaffe and we got along much better after that. I was embarrassed but he understood and he seemed to forgive me.

Corruption in the South Vietnamese Navy was endemic. Even though I met and worked with good people, I came to believe the overall system was rotten to the core. Individual commanding officers in the South Vietnamese Navy were not given commissary or other meaningful support for their units. Instead, they were given amounts of money to spend as they saw fit. I remember lots of goats, ducks and other animals purchased by the commanders being penned up on the vessels. The commanders likely purchased or purloined them from locals at more than bargain prices and then pocketed the remainder of their allowances. I began to think if I were a local, myself, I might have understandably developed some Communist tendencies.

The area we operated in was very dangerous. The Mekong Delta was full of smaller tributary waterways. Although Agent Orange had been applied in crop duster fashion around the major waterways thereby killing all vegetation within about two hundred yards of the river banks, I remember small canal-like waterways where the leaves of the trees and other tall vegetation brushed both sides of our boats as we passed through them. There was no way to turn around in such areas should we be ambushed. Such places scared the daylights out of me.

Further, if we were to be operating on larger waterways an attack upon us was not easily avoided by simply heading to the other side of the river. The other side of the river might be where the enemy wanted us to go. There might be a large underwater remote-controlled mine awaiting us. Doctrine was to stay close and duke it out at close quarters as opposed to going where Charlie might want us to go. That was often hard to do and counter-intuitive.

I should have been scared of more than that. The hazard of Agent Orange was not yet known. I remember the foul latrines at Nam Cam. Empty fifty-gallon drums clearly labeled as Agent Orange were used as toilets. They were so noxious that gas masks were made available to those using them. Periodically, the latrine barrels were doused with gasoline or kerosene and lit on fire to get rid of their noxiousness. This likely spread the Agent Orange residuals into the air for us to inhale.

It was my job to seek trouble for me and my allies. Or so I thought at first. Then I came to realize war is more like poker. You can't bet on every hand you are dealt. You need a good hand to bet on. If you don't have the right kind of cards you should fold your cards and wait on a better hand. No good poker player would ever bet on every hand. If he did, he would be a very poor poker player indeed.

When I accompanied the various South Vietnamese units on patrols, I tended to go along with my counterpart but sometimes I tended to go by myself on vessels I simply did not know well or was otherwise interested in. Or maybe I just wanted to see new areas of operations.

I became increasingly afraid as I became more aware of my vulnerability. First of all, Charlie obviously wanted me dead. Second my own allies of the South Vietnamese Navy might decide I was a liability. If I pressed my hosts too hard to complete their missions, they could quite easily kill me. They could shoot me in the confusion and noise of a fire fight or they could simply roll a grenade into the hooch where I slept. I correctly sensed I had potential threats to my life from every angle.

I became resigned to the high probability I might not survive my assignment as an advisor. I found it difficult to sleep or eat. Every single day and mission was a roll of the dice. I adopted an insulating attitude of insanity and disregard for anything except for a singular focus on my mission. I was not expecting to get out of there alive but I was not going to back off from my duties. I once read that war was basically boredom punctuated by moments of sheer terror. That was my experience. I figured war was insanity. To be sane was incongruous to it. I came to regard sanity as a precursor to death. Suffice it to say, I was shot at and I shot back. My side-arm of choice was of course my old M1 carbine.

I know people who suffered post-traumatic stress disorder (PTSD) as a result of combat in Vietnam. I did not. I give credit to at least a couple of factors: First; I was a volunteer. I had my head up when I went in. The entire venture was a lucid risk I took without any escape clause. Second; I was better prepared than most. I could speak the Vietnamese language and I very much liked the Vietnamese people. I was not as culturally isolated as some advisors in my circumstance.

In spite of deep gut-wrenching fears about dying, I never felt the cultural disconnect many others felt in a strange new country. These factors proved important to me and gave me some comfort. It was a line of mental defense for me. I had sought adventure and now I had it. I just had to deal with it.

Luckily, former President Richard M. Nixon saved me even before I arrived. In 1968, for political reasons, he had issued an edict to the effect that high-risk jobs like mine were to be "Vietnamized" or turned completely over to the Vietnamese. Implementation of the Vietnamization directive proceeded with gradually increasing impetus. My job was accordingly eliminated and I was ordered to a safer job in Saigon for the remainder of my tour. I had spent something like two months in the Mekong Delta as an advisor. When one thinks he will not survive, a couple of months is an eternity. I was very glad to get out of there alive, without a scratch on me and with my honor intact.

I subsequently reported to the Military Sealift Command in Saigon. There I joined a staff with offices on the waterfront. We supervised and supported operations involving mostly civilian contracted U.S. commercial logistic ships bringing various war supplies in-country.

I roomed in a Saigon BOQ (Bachelor Officer Quarters). It was not a comfortable accommodation. I shared a room with a marine officer from the Republic of Korea. Neither of us were competent in the other's language. Korean officers were afforded very liberal allowances for shipping up to one measurement ton of anything they wished back to South Korea upon finishing their tour of duty in Vietnam. My roommate had packed our room with a measurement ton of restaurant equipment including boxes of napkins, utensils, dishes, etc. He apparently had plans to open a restaurant when he got to go back home to South Korea. As a result, our cramped quarters were scarcely habitable. This arrangement was not the only odd thing I came to learn about the Korean military. For instance, they observed a reversed combat body count. They were not as interested in how many communists they killed. They instead carefully counted their own dead on a monthly basis. When that quota number grew too high, they simply reduced their operations accordingly. The moral of that story is do not rely on any Korean combat support towards the end of the month. Another peculiarity of Korean military folk is that they tend to prefer to drink with their own kind. They tended to co-opt bars and they did not want non-Koreans, except for Vietnamese women, to show their face in them.

Our staff worked out of an old, formerly French building located right on the waterfront where logistic ships were received, off-loaded and serviced. Our security forces of guards and sentries were mostly Chieu Hoi people meaning ex-Viet Cong soldiers. *Chieu Hoi* roughly translates to "Open Arms" in English. At the heart, the Chieu Hoi program was a psychological warfare program designed to influence scared and disgruntled Viet Cong to defect in exchange for positions provided by the South Vietnamese government. It was a successful program in that thousands of Viet Cong did in fact defect.

I took particular interest in one of our Chieu Hoi guards. He would greet us as we entered our building. He was older than I was. He had a ram-rod military posture with a distinct French flavor as he presented arms to greet us every morning with his M16 rifle. He was taller than most Vietnamese. He had a chiseled face and a slim build. His uniform was always impeccable.

He also had an obliterated and unreadable tattoo on his arm. The Vietnamese military on both sides had a tradition of tattoos. Some of the older Vietnamese veterans would have tattoos that read "*Sat Nhut*" (kill the Japanese) or "*Sat Phap*" (kill the French). Viet Cong might have a tattoo of "*Sat My*" (kill Americans). South Vietnamese and some Americans would sport "*Sat Cong*" tattoos (kill Communists). In any case, these tattoos signified a deep dedication to their cause. In theory, they could not be taken prisoner by whomever their tattoo was against.

At the time, I spoke competent Vietnamese. I began to engage him just out of curiosity about his experiences and background. He was willing to accept my interest in him. He was very open with me and we gradually became something like friends. I asked him why he defected. He was forthright in confessing his morale had been badly broken by the B-52 raids to which he was subjected as a Viet Cong soldier.

It is hard to convey the utter terror of a B-52 bombing raid. It comes as a terrible earthquake approaching from far away. The ground is already shaking but it is coming to you right now and getting worse and closer with each moment. There is nowhere to run, it is as if they know where you are and by the time you hear it coming closer to you it is too late and too broad to get around. Each 500-pound bomb is going to make its own big fish pond in front of you or on you. As the explosions get nearer to you, the wind direction changes. That is because the immense explosions are sucking the very oxygen out of the air. Soon, you can't breathe. And then you die from suffocation or the absolutely enormous and obliterating blast effect.

You don't want to do this again if you survive the first experience. As strong as you may be and no matter what your strength of belief, it will break your will. That's what happened to my Chieu Hoi friend.

My friend said he had no regrets about defecting. He had a wife and a family in Saigon. He was enjoying life with them. I began to connect with him as a human being. I would have happily killed him had I confronted him on the rivers or in the field. But then I met him and bonded with him. Once you make that transition you realize politics no longer matter as much. No matter how diametrical politics are, it is a thin veneer over the human comedy that plays out. Beneath that veneer there are real people caught up in the same unwanted and obvious struggles you are dealing with such as why are we here trying to kill one another.

Some three years later, Saigon fell to North Vietnamese communists who were entering the other side of town in Russian provided tanks. By an odd set of circumstances, I was there at that time and place in April 1975. That part of my story I will save for later in the interest of proper continuity.

A couple of anecdotal stories about my time with the Military Sealift Command in Vietnam are germane. First, is the story about a young U.S. Navy lieutenant from New Jersey. He was assigned to a Navy supply unit liaison mission with U.S. Marines up in "I Corps," meaning the northern part of South Vietnam. He wrote to his father in New Jersey to the effect the Marines were drinking warm sodas if and when they could get them. His father who apparently had control of a Coca Cola distribution franchise, approached the U.S. Navy via his congressman with a proposition: he would provide his son with refrigerators and unlimited supplies of Coca Cola if the Navy would simply get some to his son.

Somehow this was approved as a free of charge gratuity in the interest of troop morale. The Military Sea Lift Command made it happen. The Lieutenant received his refrigerators and an unlimited free supply of Coca Cola from his father for the Marines. Unfortunately, the Lieutenant succumbed to baser entrepreneurial temptations. He set up some hooches in the field with his refrigerators and cold sodas for which he charged the Marines. Soon thereafter, he staffed the hooches with young prostitutes and expanded into offering steaks, cold beer, booze and other amenities. He was soon making a lot of tax-free money up until the time he got into a bloody bar fight in Saigon and was medevaced back to the U.S.A. Someone quickly took over his operation once he left the scene. Corruption tends to be contagious when the environment is conducive and Vietnam was certainly conducive.

A second anecdote is about booze: The contracted civilian ships of the Military Sea Lift Command brought huge amounts of liquor into South Vietnam. In theory, the booze was supposed to be bound for PXes or commissary outlets and officer or enlisted clubs. I began to study what really happened when that valuable product was transported in. I found a fairly large amount was simply "lost in inventory" during the transit. In simple terms, the crews of those ships bringing it in were stealing it so as to drink it at sea or sell it on the black market when the ship arrived in Vietnam. Once the booze was off-loaded at the waterfront to the Vietnamese stevedores, another sizable quantity disappeared. The stevedores were taking their cut.

Then, the booze was loaded onto trucks for transport to the final destination. Vietnamese truck drivers then took charge of the booze. More went missing before the remainder arrived at wherever it was supposed to go. Finally, what was left arrived at some shelf in a PX or at a club bar. There a GI might buy it and then sell it on the local economy where it would be watered down.

I shared all these findings with an honorable U.S. Navy First Class Boatswains mate who worked for me. He was my direct liaison with the Vietnamese stevedores on the waterfront in Saigon. He tried to do what he could to tighten up our operations but he got death threats and I told him to back off. Sometimes you simply can't fix something that is terribly corrupt to the core, badly broken and overwhelming. The Vietnamese stevedores were essentially a mafia.

I left Vietnam for home in late 1972. My one-year tour in-country Vietnam was shorter than the remaining U.S. commitment to the war. I was on one of the last Freedom Birds coming home. I arrived at McChord Air Base when the POWs were also coming home from Hanoi. We were on the tarmac at the same time.

CHAPTER 7

Destroyer School and My Department Head Tour on USS *Schofield* (FFG-3)

I was given ample time for leave before executing orders to report to Newport, Rhode Island, for Destroyer School. Destroyer School was a six-month intensive course of study with the aim of preparing mid-grade naval officers like me to assume destroyer department head positions such as Chief Engineer Officer, Weapons Officer (in charge of all armament systems including conventional as well as nuclear arms) or Operations Officer (in charge of all information sensors as well as communication systems and operational planning).

Upon return to the United States, I endured and ignored some disrespect by anti-Vietnam war protesters in airports. Then I picked up my vehicle from a storage facility in San Diego. My vehicle was a RX-3 rotary engine Mazda. I took it from San Diego on a cross-country trip to Rhode Island. My first stop was in Las Vegas. I had time to enjoy myself and I had some money on me as result of my time in Vietnam.

My favorite casino in Las Vegas was and remains Benny Binion's Horseshoe Casino on the old Las Vegas Strip. I pulled up to it and the concierge had a valet park my car under the casino. I liked that casino because it had one deck blackjack shoes that favored an amateur but avid gambler like me.

As I checked into the casino, I got very sick right away. I had brought back with me some malady from Vietnam. It may have been malaria as evidenced by several recurrences I later suffered over subsequent years. I was sick a lot when I was in-country. I was young and strong with a good immune system, so I was usually able to bounce back quickly. My maladies in Vietnam were often vaguely diagnosed as insect-delivered, bad water or simply an unknown viral infection. My treatments relied heavily on APCs (all-purpose capsules) and quinine water which Navy corpsmen prescribed for just about everything.

I checked into my room in the casino and put a wet washcloth on my head to alleviate my fever. There was a knock on my door. It was a young woman wondering if I would like to party. The concierge had obviously pegged me as a returning Vietnam veteran probably looking for a good time. I explained to the young woman I was dying and to go away. The concierge figured she was not my type and sent a parade of other ladies for my consideration. Finally, I bummed some aspirin from a couple of them, for which I tipped them extravagantly, and sent them back to the concierge with a message to cease and desist. It was two or three days before I could lift my head off my sweat-soaked pillow.

When I began to feel better, I proceeded to lose considerably more money in the casino. Finally, I called for my car and drove eastward on my long journey to Rhode Island. About 200 miles into the desert the rotary engine in my car burned up. A very mercenary cowboy offered to tow me back the nearest Mazda dealership in Las Vegas for about a dollar a mile (a very steep price in the 1970s). I spent another week in Las Vegas while I waited for the engine to be replaced in my vehicle. Meanwhile, I continued to lose more money on the craps and blackjack tables. I began to wish I was back in Vietnam.

Finally, after driving across the country I arrived in Newport, Rhode Island. There I met my future wife, Marlene. Marlene was and still is an attractive red-haired girl from Connecticut. She was working in Newport for Salve Regina College (now University) which was her Alma Mater. We met one another at one of the officer clubs known as the Datum. It was a hangout for junior officers. I was quietly sipping bourbon at the bar. Unlike me, I did not gently hit on her but instead just sat there at the bar next to her sipping my nectar. Maybe I was playing hard to get or maybe I was simply feeling mellow. After a long pause, she asked me to talk to her in as much as she was waiting for her friend to finish some sort of personal business with another naval officer. So, I talked to her. We dated for the entire six months of my Destroyer School course.

Students at the Destroyer School studied a specific and modern class of destroyer in great detail. I scored very high in all my studies, but I did best in terms of propulsion engineering. I hoped I would be assigned as Chief Engineer Officer on a destroyer type ship. To date, most of my experience at sea had been weapons related. If I were assigned as a Chief Engineer Officer, it would have helped me in terms of gaining a better potential shot at eventually commanding a destroyer. Nevertheless, the needs of the Navy dictated everything. The powers that be chose to build upon my past strengths and I was given orders to report to USS *Schofield* (FFG-3) as her new Weapons Officer.

This was not a step backwards nor sideways in terms of my career progression. *Schofield* was a desirable modern ship based in San Diego. She was equipped with a considerable weapons battery. She had a powerful SM-2 Standard missile battery capable of engaging substantial air threats as well as surface threats, a 5-inch, .38-caliber gun and the most modern ASW suite in the Navy including an ASROC (Anti-Submarine Rocket System) that included nuclear weapons capability. As Weapons Officer, I was also the

USS *Schofield* (FFG-3), my third ship

Nuclear Weapons Officer which involved a great deal of rigid adherence to very strict standards in training and maintenance. Inspections were tough and exacting. Failure to pass those nuclear weapon inspections was potentially career ending.

Schofield's SQS-26 sonar system was state of the art and much more advanced than the systems I had supervised on *Laffey*. Given I was the Weapons Officer, I was in charge of the various fire control radars associated with the missile and gun batteries. I was also in charge of the very modern three-dimensional radar that my missile battery relied upon.

Schofield also had a telescoping type of hangar for a helicopter and a smallish flight deck. Those facilities were my turf when a helicopter detachment was not embarked. When deployed, we hosted an embarked Sea King Sikorsky helicopter detachment. The Sea King was basically a lighter naval version of the Army Black Hawk helicopter except for her advanced Electronic Naval Warfare suite and considerable ASW systems.

Schofield had a modern pressure-fired boiler which was at times problematic. The boiler provided 1200-pound steam to our propulsion system. Her top speed was something like 31 knots.

Schofield had some 300 souls in her crew of which some 90 or so reported to me. What distinguished her as a frigate as opposed to a destroyer was the fact that she had a single propulsion screw as opposed to two. As with *Laffey*, *Schofield* typically accompanied and screened aircraft carriers.

When I joined *Schofield* in 1973, she was operating in the far-away Indian Ocean. I left Southern California embarked on USS *Niagara Falls* (AFS-3), a combat stores supply ship which was bound for the Indian Ocean. It was a long, slow and somewhat boring transit. To pass the time, I volunteered to stand watches driving the ship as Officer of the Deck. It was still rather mundane compared to being on a destroyer or a frigate although we did re-supply some ships at sea.

While I was embarked on the USS *Niagara Falls*, I made a casual acquaintance with a Chief Warrant Officer and communications specialist who was assigned to the ship as the communications officer. His name was John Walker. We met because we sometimes took meals together in the wardroom. Unbeknownst to me as well as just about anyone in the U.S. Navy at that time, John Walker was actively spying for the Soviet Union. I do not recall much of anything notable or remarkable about John Walker except for the fact he was rather nondescript and he had a slightly creepy air about him.

Walker eventually headed a spy ring of four Navy people including his older brother LCDR Walter Walker, USN; Senior Chief Petty Officer (Radioman) Jerry Whitworth; and John Walker's son Michael Walker, a seaman working on the aircraft carrier USS *Nimitz*. During his time as a Soviet spy, Walker helped the Soviets decipher more than one million encrypted naval messages. *The New York Times* reported in 1987 the spy operation "is sometimes described as the most damaging Soviet spy ring in history."

The Soviets had intercepted our coded messages, but they had never been able to read them. With Walker providing the code cards, this was one half, of what they needed to read them. The other half they needed were the cipher machines themselves. Though Walker could give them repair manuals, he could not give them the machines. Within a month of John Walker volunteering his spy services, the Soviets arranged, through the North Koreans, to hijack a U.S. Navy ship with its cipher machines. In early 1968 the USS *Pueblo* (AGER-2), an environmental research ship attached to U.S. Naval intelligence as a spy ship, was seized and taken into Wonsan Harbor where the cipher machines were quickly removed and flown to Moscow. Now Moscow had both parts of the puzzle. They had the machine and they also had an American spy in place in Norfolk with access to the code cards.

Things quickly unraveled for John Walker in November 1984 when his ex-wife contacted the Boston FBI office reporting him as spying for the Soviet Union. She was fearful her children might become involved in the spy ring. She did not then know that her son Michael had already become an active participant; she later admitted she would not have reported the spy ring had she known her son was involved.

Electronic surveillance of John Walker was authorized by the Foreign Intelligence Court. On May 19, 1985 Walker left his house in Norfolk and was followed covertly by a team of FBI agents to the Washington, D.C., area. Later that evening about 8:30 PM he drove to a rural area in Montgomery County, Maryland, where he was seen placing a package in a wooded area near a "No Hunting" sign. The FBI retrieved the package which was found to have 124 pages of classified information stolen from the USS *Nimitz*, where Walker's son Michael was assigned.

Walker was arrested during the early morning hours of May 20, 1985, at a motel in Montgomery County, Maryland, by FBI agents who telephoned his motel room and told him his car had been hit in an accident. He was apprehended when he came out of his room.

Due to an odd combination of circumstances, I happened to be fishing in the Occoquan River in Virginia on Saturday, May 19, 1985 with an FBI agent friend who was a next-door neighbor in our townhouse complex in Springfield, Virginia. Before going on our fishing trip, he told me we would have to leave early and quickly return home if he received a certain telephone call on his mobile telephone. The place we were fishing apparently had poor reception but eventually the call did come. We left quickly and returned home where my friend got in his car and left without an explanation. I later learned he had been on the team of FBI agents who apprehended John Walker.

John Walker cooperated to some degree with authorities, enough to form a plea bargain that reduced the sentence for his son, Michael, to 25 years. All other members of the spy ring received more than life in prison sentences.

Finally, going back to my time aboard USS *Niagara Falls*, where I met John Walker, we had a rendezvous with my ship USS *Schofield* which we resupplied. I was transferred from the *Niagara Falls* to the *Schofield* via high-line meaning the two ships pulled up next to one another while underway, I sat in a metal chair that was passed from one ship to the other via a manila high-line. My scant baggage then came behind me by similar means.

I came aboard and in quick succession met my new Executive Officer, the Commanding Officer and the Weapons Officer I was to relieve. Not too long afterwards we visited the unspoiled Seychelles, islands off the east coast of Africa, which I think was the most beautiful place I have ever been. The Seychelles were once owned by the French who imprinted their culinary traditions and later by the English who imprinted their language. The beautiful black sand beaches and the lush tropical environment of the place completed the picture. It was like Hawaii must have been at some point. The population consisted mostly of black creole people.

After the visit to the Seychelles, we completed our deployment and returned to San Diego via the Western Pacific stopping in Singapore, Hong Kong and the Philippines. Shortly after arriving in San Diego, the commanding officer was relieved by a new commanding officer. One of my biggest challenges on *Schofield* was presented by the new commanding officer. He was autocratic and tyrannical. At first, we seemed to get along, but our relations became progressively problematic. He was a brilliant nuclear power trained engineer who always wore a slide-rule on his belt. I was amazed at how he could analyze complex systems at a glance and instantly see things I could not. I needed more time.

I was the Senior Watch Officer in addition to other positions and duties I had on the ship. As such, I was in charge of training officer watch standers and recommending them for certifications granted by the commanding officer. Soon after the new commanding officer took command, I briefed him on the status of our watch organization. At the time we had a four-section in-port watch team meaning an officer could expect to spend every fourth day and night on duty in port. I was proud to tell him we were ready to go to a five-section watch section as the result of my assiduous efforts to train the watch standers.

He told me we would have a three-section watch team for the entire ship both in port and at sea and to make it happen right away. That was terrible news particularly to the married officers and crewmen. A three-section watch team meant nobody ever had a full weekend free of duty while the ship was in port. We were preparing for another deployment and those weekends were important as we were preparing to leave loved ones. At sea, a three-section watch was exhausting in terms of sleep deprivation.

The new Commanding Officer also decreed that no movies would henceforth be shown in the wardroom. Officers would instead be expected to read technical manuals in their off time. This was also bad news in that movies were about our only real diversion at sea where our life was rather grueling.

I sucked all that up. Then I realized the fullness of his personal style of leadership. He would call me to his cabin and give me orders about certain things he wanted me to do. Like a good and professional sailor, I would listen to his orders and say, "Aye, aye, Sir!" which means I understand and I will comply. The discourse was not over at that point. He would then take long minutes telling me in excruciating detail what he would do to me if I did not execute his orders perfectly. I also came to understand he expected me to let shit flow freely downhill. He wanted me to communicate to my subordinates the way he communicated to me. I refused to do so. I was determined to be the buffer between him and the people who worked for me. Once he realized that, our relations declined further.

The thing I remember most saliently about that cruise was our role in Operation Frequent Wind. That operation was mostly a humanitarian rescue operation occasioned by the fall of South Vietnam.

In April, 1975, we were bobbing around in the South China Sea. Because I had Vietnamese language skills, powers from above plucked me from my ship and had me transferred via helicopter to the Saigon waterfront along with a trusted senior petty officer whom I selected from others who worked for me. Preparation time was very scant. The petty officer was an FTM1: a first-class petty officer missile fire control specialist. We went in with two changes of uniform clothing and with only .45-caliber pistols on our belts. As we flew in, we were going against the tide of the South Vietnamese aircraft fleeing South Vietnam. At that time South Vietnam had the fourth largest air force in the world behind the Soviet Union, the USA and China. Everything that could fly was in the air trying to get out of South Vietnam.

My orders were to take control of three South Vietnamese Navy ships awaiting me on the waterfront. These ships were medium to large amphibious ships called LSILs (Landing Ship Infantry Large). They were absolutely packed with refugees including women, children of various ages and crewmen assigned to the ships. My orders were to take them to sea and bring them to the Republic of the

Philippines. On the way there, I was to render their armament unusable and then recommission the vessels as U.S. Navy vessels to comply with diplomatic arrangements with the Government of the Philippines.

I knew the Saigon waterfront well and was able to coach our helicopter pilot exactly where to take us. When I was deposited on the Saigon waterfront, I was coincidentally in sight of where my Chieu Hoi friend and I had been together in the Military Sealift Command some two years before. I knew he was no longer there. I had no time to waste in any case. Saigon was literally falling right then. I had to take those ships to sea right away. Nor could I spend time doing anything for him except wondering about what was going to happen to him. His options were likely grim. The North Vietnamese had lists of people to kill. He was almost assuredly on such a list. I guess he was either executed quickly or perhaps he ended his days more slowly in a re-education camp. I never found out what became of him.

One of the three ships I was ordered to take to sea could not get underway under her own power. We had to take her in tow with the ship I was embarked upon. That ship was the *Loi Cong*. We hastily put to sea.

At least a few things worried me. First, I wished I had had the foresight to get some good weather forecasts before I left *Schofield*. The ships were so full of refugees there was no room for everyone to go below decks. If we hit bad weather at sea it could have been disastrous. I simply did not know what conditions were like until I arrived aboard those ships. I also correctly worried the ships were very dirty with heroin. Whatever South Vietnamese currency the people had was now worthless. The logical thing to do was get rid of their money before embarking by turning it into something smaller but valuable. A logical choice was heroin. Later, I found what appeared might be valuable works of Vietnamese art stashed on the ship I was riding. Finally, I worried I did not know who was embarked. I would be needing to report things like that to my U.S. Navy authorities.

The Vietnamese captain of the ship I was riding had introduced himself as the senior Vietnamese officer afloat among the three ships. He lied to me. I noticed a rather dapper guy in civilian clothing when we ate meals together in the wardroom. Everyone near him seemed to defer to him. I came to learn he was a three-star South Vietnamese army general: a province commander. I gathered he was the one who brought aboard the purloined artwork. I radioed his biographical data as best I knew it to U.S. Navy authorities.

I tried to get a head count of how many people were on those ships, but I gave up. I don't think the Vietnamese officers knew the number either. I estimated I was bringing in some 500 souls into the Philippines.

Once the opportunity presented itself, I assembled the more senior South Vietnamese officers. I introduced myself and informed them of my orders including the need to disable their larger guns by removing their breech blocks and throwing them overboard. I told them the petty officer I had brought aboard with me would supervise and certify that effort. I informed them I was ordered to recommission their vessels as U.S. Navy ships in accordance with diplomatic arrangements with the government of the Philippines. I went on to say they could conduct whatever ceremonies they thought appropriate when their flags were lowered before they raised the U.S. flag over their vessels. I also let them know they would be delivered to a camp on Grande Island in Subic Bay in the Philippines. There they would be processed, given civilian clothing, decent quarters and other humanitarian support as needed. They were quite cordial and accepting. A few stepped up to me to deliver their personal sidearms. I wish they had not done that in as some of those pistols looked like family heirlooms such as pearl-handled revolvers. They had put me in the difficult position of having to throw their handguns overboard.

Their ceremonies upon lowering their national colors were touching and very dignified if brief. Some were crying as their colors were lowered. We proceeded to Grande Island without incident or bad weather. After three days at sea, everybody was transferred to Grande Island which theretofore had been a pleasant R & R facility for U.S. Navy folks from the Subic Bay Navy Base. It had been transmogrified into a rather orderly albeit crowded refugee tent city.

Curiously, Grande Island had an old U.S. Army gun installation that was kind of a curio. It dated from the Spanish American War. I have reason to believe my great uncle Carl Ossendott may have manned that gun installation sometime in the years before WWI. I knew he was stationed in the Philippines before WWI as a coastal artilleryman, but he was now dead and I was never able to verify exactly where he had served.

Meanwhile, my ship *Schofield* had been at sea taking aboard helicopter after helicopter laden with refugees. The larger helicopters would hover over our small flight deck where they would discharge their human cargo. Then they would ditch near the ship and the pilots would swim to the ship. The smaller Huey type helicopters would land on the ship briefly and then be pushed over the side into the water. The sky was full of aircraft waiting their turn to ditch near the ship.

I had been trying to kill the yellow man for some time. I felt my rescue efforts with the refugees balanced my record. I brought back many more Vietnamese who became productive fellow Americans than I ever aspired to kill. That was by far the best thing I ever accomplished in my time in Vietnam. The U.S. Army General Officer in Tactical Command of Operation Frequent Wind graciously gave me a special citation of commendation and I later received a Humanitarian Service Medal as did the petty officer who accompanied me on the mission.

Back aboard the *Schofield*, I went ashore one evening and had dinner at a Filipino restaurant in Olongapo, a town adjacent to the naval base. My starter course was of *baluts*. *Baluts* are definitely an acquired taste. The balut is a fertilized duck egg which is boiled and then buried in sand for some amount of time until it becomes somewhat addled and smelly. Luckily, it tastes much better than it smells. The embryo duck inside is half formed and sort of crunchy. Most non-native people refuse to even try them, but I did. I like them. The first time I tried one was in a bar in Olongapo. A Filipino band was playing. I remember they stopped playing when I ate my first balut. They were interested in observing my reaction. As I have mentioned, I am adventurous.

Post script: A good number of years after the fall of Vietnam, I met a younger Vietnamese optometrist in Avon, Connecticut. I used my waning Vietnamese language skills to ask him about where he grew up and how he came to America. He said he grew up in a smaller village near Saigon. He went on to say he and his family fled Vietnam about the time Saigon fell. He was about five years old at the time. A few more details established that I had likely brought him and his family to the Philippines. As we talked, he became a little emotional and so did I.

The *Schofield* visited a good number of ports in the Western Pacific. The ship also performed well in a very prolonged, exhausting war game exercise. By the end of the exercise, I was so utterly sleep starved I could only be roused to stand my watches with considerable difficulty. Not long afterward, *Schofield's* deployment came to an end, and we proceeded back to our homeport in San Diego via Pearl Harbor in Hawaii.

Marlene and I had been keeping up an active correspondence. We decided to get married in Southern California. We had close friends living in Beverly Hills: David Lloyd and his wife Arline. Arline and my wife Marlene grew up in the same small New England town of Thomaston, Connecticut. David spent four years in the Navy before beginning a long and successful career in television comedy writing. He is probably best remembered for his work on *The Tonight Show, Mary Tyler Moore, Taxi* and *Cheers.* We asked David and Arline to stand up for us at what was intended to be a small wedding ceremony at the courthouse. They had a better idea. We were married in an outdoor military ceremony at their home

My wedding, 1976

on August 7, 1976. Most of my wardroom colleagues participated in the ceremony as our wedding party.

After the wedding, Marlene and I spent our honeymoon at the opulent Santa Barbara Biltmore Hotel. Even before we checked in, I got sick again with what I imagine was another severe bout of malaria. It lasted a few days and ruined our honeymoon.

CHAPTER 8

Duty As an Exchange Officer in the *Armada de Argentina* (Argentine Navy)

As my tour of duty on *Schofield* was coming to an end, I became aware of an interesting opportunity to serve as a Personnel Exchange Officer in the *Armada de Argentina* (Argentine navy) for two years. I was intrigued by that possibility. It was another opportunity to be adventurous. It might likely have been a sideways step in my career progression, but I was interested in it. So, I volunteered for it and was accepted. Marlene agreed.

In preparation for that posting, I was given orders to once again report to the Defense Language Institute in pleasant Monterey, California for six months of Spanish language training. The Navy, in its wisdom, invited Marlene to attend that training with me. We found a comfortable apartment in Monterey and settled in.

I am not necessarily talented in language study, but I had picked up some handy methods during my earlier study of Vietnamese. The language institute uses an "immersion" technique meaning one cannot use any English after the first week of study. I found I could learn a lot more vocabulary than was normally assigned (typically about 40 new words a day). I took to carrying a bunch of 3x5 cards in my shirt pocket. I wrote down every new vocabulary word I heard or was otherwise exposed to on my 3x5 card. On the reverse side I would write the English meaning of the word. I would review them daily. When I had the word down, I would put the card aside. By this means, I was able to at least double my vocabulary comprehension while at the same time reducing the number of cards in my shirt pocket by transferring them to the large stack I had carefully saved on my home desk.

We completed our language studies in April of 1977. We arrived in Buenos Aires shortly thereafter. Buenos Aires, and Argentina in general, is a wonderful place to be. I took to it right away. While in Buenos Aires, my wife and I were hosted by several U.S. Navy officers as well as officers from the Army and Air Force assigned to the joint U.S. Military Group or the U.S. Embassy. I was also processed into the Argentine Navy at their headquarters in Buenos Aires where I was given an Argentine navy identification card. That card was invaluable. It was basically a "get out of jail free" card.

At that time, Argentina was ruled by a military junta which had overthrown the government led by Isabela Perón (second wife and widow of Juan Perón) who was placed under house arrest. Meanwhile, Argentina was embroiled in a "dirty war." An extreme leftist group called the Montoneros was conducting a serious insurgency effort against the government. It was mostly an urban war with lots of murders and bombings.

While I was being processed into the Argentine navy, I was interviewed by a younger Argentine rear admiral. He told me I would be initially assigned to Argentina's only aircraft carrier, the ARA *Veinticinco de Mayo*. He went on to say if and when I wished to be assigned to any other unit, I simply needed to call him and he would make it happen. I told him I would wish to embark on a variety of Argentine ships so as to maximize my experience. He smiled and said, "Call me."

After a week or so in Buenos Aires becoming familiar with the

U.S. Embassy, we traveled by train to what would become home for the next two years. The naval base of Puerto Belgrano is adjacent to the smaller, pleasant town of Punta Alta. The latitude is roughly the same as that of Washington, D.C., except in the opposite hemisphere of course. The seasons, although reversed, were like that of Washington, D.C., except a good deal drier. We were in the Provincia de Buenos Aires but basically within the Pampas area of Argentina, a decidedly rural cattle, sunflower seed and grain area. It looked a lot like Kansas.

The naval base was very comfortable and offered many amenities: a movie Theater, clay tennis courts, a golf course, horse stables, swimming pools and water skiing available for the asking.

Centered on the base grounds stood an elegant old military hotel where we lived and boarded with numerous Argentine officers and their families for several months before our household goods arrived. The hotel was a bit austere: just three skinny single beds, a closet, a mirror on the wall and some bureau drawers in our room but we did have a private bathroom. The bathroom also served as a laundry area rigged with pulleys and ropes to be able to hang clothes to dry. We ate and socialized with Argentine officers and their families in a grand dining area on the first floor. That was an important feature for us because we got to meet and begin friendships with a lot of people.

Among our first contacts was a young attractive couple to which we quickly became quite close. The husband, Carlos (not his real name), was of my rank. Like me, he was a surface warfare officer but also with a sub-specialty in intelligence. He was also the Argentine equivalent of a SEAL. His wife was of first-generation Hungarian descent. They had two younger children. I choose not to disclose the true name of "Carlos" for reasons that will become clearer later.

Life in the hotel was generally pleasant but the social atmosphere was somewhat formal. Men wore civilian suits with ties and women usually wore dresses and high heels at dinner. The food was good and the Argentine wines excellent. A few months after our arrival, our shipment of household goods arrived and Marlene and I were assigned a comfortable but modest house on the base.

The neighborhood around our house was populated by midgrade Argentine naval officers with young families. Marlene and I socially integrated very well among these families. One of my personal diplomatic initiatives was to introduce the mint julep. That was very enthusiastically received. Unfortunately, bourbon was very scarce in Argentina. But, good Argentine brandy was abundant. So, I resorted to the antebellum mint julep recipe which called for brandy instead of bourbon.

A Kentucky uncle had gifted me a set of silver mint julep goblets as a wedding gift. We pressed them into service over and over again. Crushed ice, a little water, some mulled mint leaves, confectioners' sugar and a good amount of brandy, then the concoction was stirred until the silver goblet frosted. Soon my neighbors were talking about building a statue dedicated to me and the flower strewn path to conviviality I had introduced them to via the mint julep. The statue never materialized but I do still appreciate the sentiment.

We also introduced the concept of Halloween to the neighborhood children. Argentines do not celebrate Halloween but once we gave them a bit of encouragement, we had kids dressed up in imaginative costumes knocking on our door seeking candy.

I guess our efforts at personal diplomacy were successful in as much as I was asked to assume the role of *Papá Noel* (Santa Claus) when Christmas came around. Our neighbors thought my accent to be appropriate and perhaps more authentic. Seasons are reversed in the Southern hemisphere. Christmas is in the middle of their summer. Nonetheless, I donned the traditional red and white sweltering garb and beard of Santa Claus. A French built Alluette helicopter of the Argentine navy placed me and my big bag of gifts among a throng of Argentine youngsters on the naval base.

I did my duty to the best of my ability but my helicopter was called away for another tasking. Some thoughtful Argentine officer commandeered a cherry picker truck to rescue me. I left the throng of children waving from the bucket of the cherry picker. Somehow, that worked for both the assembled family members and the children.

Shortly after we moved into our house on the naval base, we hired a part-time maid who came to the house twice a week or so. Her name was María Eugenia. She was a wonderful salt-of-the-earth country woman. She was short and stout and mother to a rather large family who lived in a neat but dirt floored house in the adjoining town.

I remember having a conversation with her that went like this: "We had some guests over last night. We were playing some games and one of them lost a die. I could not find it but it may be under our sofa. Please let me know if you find it." I was speaking to her in Spanish. I confused the word for die (*dado*) with the quite similar word for finger (*dedo*). In other words, I was telling her someone lost a finger last night and it might be under the sofa. She took that aboard but I could tell it bothered her. She was likely contemplating about the strange games North Americans might play.

The ship to which I was initially assigned, the aircraft carrier ARA *Veinticinco de Mayo* was an older ship having been built by the Royal Navy and subsequently modernized by the Dutch navy who angled the flight deck after WWII. It was smaller than a typical U.S. Navy carrier, but it was a capable ship with A-4 attack aircraft, S-2 Tracker ASW aircraft and helicopters of a couple of types. I could literally walk to her either from the base hotel or our house.

I rotated around the ship from one department to another becoming familiar with all aspects of the ship and her airwing as well as the customs and ways of doing business in a navy to which I was just becoming accustomed. I spent a fair amount of time at sea with her as we conducted air operations in the South Atlantic. Once I felt I had my sea legs, I called the Admiral in Buenos Aires and asked to be assigned to the cruiser ARA *General Belgrano* (ex-cruiser USS *Phoenix*). The cruiser had a total of 1,500 or so officers and crew. I was assigned as officer in charge of one of her

The aircraft carrier ARA *Veinticinco de Mayo*

five 6-inch, .47-caliber gun turrets each of which had three guns for a total of 15 main guns on the ship.

The ARA *General Belgrano* was the oldest ship I ever served on in my Navy career. Her keel was laid down in 1935. She was old but very well maintained. Stepping into my gun turret was like stepping into a time machine and being transported back to 1935. Everything that could be shined inside the turret, e.g., brass or copper, was buffed and polished by the gunner mates until they gleamed. Her guns were very accurate as well. The first time I saw the guns in action was when we conducted a shore bombardment in the south Atlantic coast of Argentina. I turned my turret over to my assistant turret officer and went ashore via boat to spot and observe the fall of fire. I was quite impressed by the power and accuracy of the guns.

The Argentine officers were warming to me. Unlike the U.S. Navy, Argentine ships were more civilized. They had bars aboard where we did a lot of socializing before and after meals. The Argentine officers had a peculiar sense of humor. They enjoyed putting people in potentially embarrassing situations just to see how they would react. Sometimes I would belly up to the bar in the wardroom only to note a small card proclaiming, "Drinks are on Lieutenant Hall. The drink of the evening is _____." The name of the drink would be whatever Spanish word I had butchered badly that day. I would just smile and gladly pay the bar tab for anyone who wished to enjoy my hospitality. That appeared to have been the correct response based upon the reaction of my Argentine shipmates. They enjoyed seeing a bit of grace under pressure. In turn, I appreciated their efforts to improve my Spanish. I never butchered the same word more than once. My Spanish improved.

(The ARA *General Belgrano* was later sunk by the British Royal Navy submarine HMS *Conqueror* during the Falklands/Malvinas War. I lost a number of good shipmates when that happened. Included was the Chief Engineer Officer of the ARA *General Belgrano* whom I regarded as a personal friend.)

The cruiser ARA *General Belgrano*

Among the many things I enjoyed in Argentina was hunting. I got deep into hunting there. I was living in a sportsman's paradise. The area teemed with game: five kinds of deer, three kinds of game birds, red stag elk, huge Russian boar, black buck (an imported type of antelope from India), large native rhea as well as uncountable numbers of European hare plus a peculiar and delicious tasting large rodent-like animal with all white meat about the size of a badger called *vizcacha*, not to mention a smaller, tasty armadillo called *peludo*. When baked in its shell it looked a lot like a lobster but tasted like pork.

The bird hunting was phenomenal. It was not out of the ordinary for me to shoot fifty partridge in one day with my Argentine friends. Because I was shooting so many birds, I had to carry a sea-bag as a game bag. These were smaller quail-sized birds called *perdice* in Spanish. We mostly hunted them around the vast fields of sunflower plantings where their populations grew in geometric progressions given the plentitude of food. Two other larger birds were available, but I preferred the *perdice* for their better flavor. The typical Argentine method of preparation was to pluck them, cook them and then pickle them in *escabeche* (oil, vinegar and herbs).

One aspect of the bird hunt that I loved was the *asado* or barbeque. About midday, we would pause at some shady place. My friend Garcia, a very classy kind of guy, taught me how to do it right. He would start a fire using a special hardwood called *quebracho*, something like mesquite. He would produce a card table, silverware, a checkered tablecloth and several bottles of good Argentine Malbec red wine. It was my job to bring the cigars and good whiskey purchased from the U.S. Embassy commissary for after dinner. We would feast upon short ribs and Italian style fresh bread in an extended slow afternoon gorging.

Speaking of *asados*, I went to very many. It is a typical Argentine culinary experience often lasting most of a day. It starts off with appetizers called *achuras*. These usually consist of *chorizo* or *morcilla* (blood) sausages, small intestines grilled crispy like bacon

Hunting in Argentina

and thick grilled slices of provolone cheese. Then comes the main course of short ribs. Many Argentine houses have a special outdoor building just for hosting *asados.*

I came to love the Argentine people as I assimilated into their culture. Most of the Argentines I met via their navy were urbane people the majority from Buenos Aires. But I particularly enjoyed the more primitive and basic gaucho types I met in the countryside when I was hunting. They were truly a genuine, memorable salt-of-the-earth type people who reminded me of my Kentucky friends and kin.

Argentina is a cultural melting pot very much like the U.S.A. All kinds of people settled there and constituted the ethnic make-up of the country. Italians, Germans, Greeks, Russians, Irish, etc.

When I was in Argentina, I remember learning that about 60 percent of Argentines had an Italian last name. Twelve percent had a German last name. There were villages near the Andes Mountains to the west that were entirely German speaking. The City of Puerto Madryn on the east coast of Argentina was settled almost entirely by Welsh people.

Unlike Brazil, Argentina has very few black people. I met only one in the small town near the naval base. His nickname translated to "snow flake" in English. I suppose Argentines might have been judged as somewhat racist if viewed from a North American perspective at that time. While I was there, the U.S. Marine Corps stopped assigning black Marines to be embassy guards. The blacks complained about being the subjects of photo opportunities in the streets of Buenos Aires. In my view, the Argentines were simply unfamiliar with blacks and they were intrigued by them. Unfortunately, this caused discomfort on the part of the Marines. This situation would probably not exist today.

* * * *

Boar hunting: I tried hard to successfully hunt boar but I ultimately failed to kill one. These were not feral pigs but rather true Russian Boar which could weigh more than 500 pounds. I hunted them in a couple of ways. One way was on horseback with a special breed of dog called a *Dogo Argentino.* A Dogo was a mix of Great Dane (for size), hound (for smell tracking) and bull dog (for a firm biting grip on the boar).

I had ridden a bit when I was a kid growing up in Kentucky. I was, however, way out of shape for a day in the saddle in my early thirties in Argentina. Nor was I agile enough to do the things the gauchos could do while mounted on a horse. For my first effort at hunting in this manner, I carried a .45-caliber pistol on my belt. My gaucho hosts did not want me to use it for fear of me killing one of their precious *Dogos.* They used knives only and they preferred I follow suit. Their knives were large, flashy bowie-knife-like things called *facóns*. I have a smaller version of such a knife on the wall of my man cave today. The blade is steel with a silver and gold inlaid hasp and handle. The dogs would immobilize the boar and then the gaucho would lean off his horse and into the melee. He would slit the throat of the boar without dismounting. I was not yet ready nor brave enough to attempt this so on my first hunt I decided to observe. I witnessed a large boar kill a horse by getting under it and then disemboweling the horse with its large and sharp tusks. Frankly, I was never brave enough to try and kill a boar with a knife.

The other way I hunted boar was by scouting watering holes meant for cattle (typically served by smaller windmills to bring the water up). When we found recent or otherwise promising signs of boar tracks or activity near the water holes, we would set up an ambush site for the night. Boar tend mostly to nocturnal activity.

On perhaps the worst night I have ever experienced outside of Vietnam, I had some Argentine friends drop me off near a very remote water hole deep in the Pampas where I wanted to hunt. It was winter and exceedingly cold. They dropped me off and then proceeded to some other place they wanted to hunt. I carried a rifle, a good knife, a rather heavy car battery in a backpack to power a search light I had taped to the barrel of my rifle and little else except for a thermos bottle of hot strong tea called *yerba mate* and perhaps a flask of Dutch gin favored by Argentines. I may have had some snacks in my backpack as well.

This was before the days of cell phones. My friends and I simply agreed I would be picked up the next morning. I proceeded to walk to the watering hole maybe two kilometers away. As I crossed an iced over stream on the way there, the ice broke and I went in up to my chest. I didn't lose anything except for my breath. I struggled out of the stream bed with some difficulty. My wet clothing froze quickly. I realized I was in trouble. With my teeth chattering I arrived at the watering hole. I decided the hunt was ruined and I focused upon building a fire.

The trouble was that this was in the pampas where little but scrub brush and pampas grass grows. The Pampas has very few trees. The only fuel I could find was dried cow flops. They burned rather inefficiently and without giving off much heat but it was about all I had. I spent the night gathering cow flops and feeding the fire to stay kind of warm.

Boar did in fact approach. They obviously smelled me or saw my fire. They circled around me. I could hear their piglets squealing as they investigated my presence. Boars are extremely intelligent and they have excellent sensory abilities. They left in fairly quick order.

Then as I sat near my measly cow flop fire trying to keep warm, I sensed an animal near me. I turned on the spotlight taped to my rifle barrel and saw bright orange eyes looking at me. It was a large cougar or mountain lion. I was not interested in anything at that point beyond keeping warm. I shooed it away. It was not interested in me except in terms of what I imagined was curiosity. I don't think I slept at all that miserable night. At first light, I set off for my rendezvous with my hunting comrades taking care to find a safer crossing point across the frozen stream. I was so glad when they picked me up.

Another brief Argentine hunting story: I was after European red stag (elk) in the Pampas. I was on foot scouting when I saw a young gaucho riding on a horse on the other side of a fence which separated two *estancias* (very large ranch properties). I engaged him in conversation. I seemed to scare him. I was bearded, wearing an old jungle green uniform from my time in Vietnam and I was carrying a military Argentine Mauser rifle. I spoke Spanish with an accent. Argentina was embroiled in a continuing insurgency war. No wonder he was afraid of me. I imagine he quickly told his supervisor or perhaps the landowner of his encounter with me. In any case the local gendarmes wasted little time in finding me. They took me and my Argentine hunting buddy into custody and brought us back to their rural headquarters for questioning.

As mentioned earlier, my Argentine military ID card as well as my official U.S. passport were like get-out-of-jail free cards. I then watched Argentine police work at its best. The gendarmes had a dilemma. On one hand they had to appear responsive to the estancia owner who sicced them on us. On the other hand, they knew we were harmless and in fact very well credentialed. Their solution to the dilemma was brilliant. They prepared a wonderfully slow, wine-drenched *asado* for us. That way they could tell the landowner they had detained us for an eight-hour interview.

One more hunting story: an Argentine companion and I were hunting deer on a large "*estancia*" or ranch. Towards the middle of the day, we decided to return to a modest house where the *postero* or ranch-hand overseer of a section of the estancia lived. As we approached his house, we found him next to a pickup truck. He was standing over a large squealing domestic pig he had trussed up and tied with coat hanger wire. The pig was too large for him to lift and place in his pickup truck. He asked for our assistance and we agreed to help him. We lifted the pig onto the bed of his truck with its head hanging off the end of the tail gate. The field hand produced a large aluminum pan partially filled with rock salt crystals. I deduced he was going to make *morcilla*. I enjoyed eating morcilla, which is made from pig blood and cooked rice and then stuffed into small intestine casings. I had never seen it made so we stayed with him to watch the process.

He made a small incision into the jugular vein of the pig. As the blood came spurting out, he slowly stirred it into the pan with the rock salt. Things were going smoothly until the pig began to die. It then vomited into the pan. The field hand just shrugged his shoulders and smiled as he continued stirring. I lost my taste for morcilla for some time afterwards but I later forgave the field hand and began to eat it again when I could get the smell and thought of pig vomit out of my mind.

Later that afternoon, I relaxed on the back porch of the *postero's* house. I was sitting there sipping a nice Argentine red wine. A huge tarantula was moving across the yard. The width of the spider was at least eleven inches or so, way too big to cover with my hat had I wished to do that. As I watched with interest, a large rooster was also eyeing the spider. The rooster ran up to the spider. The spider reared up to defend itself but the rooster was not intimidated. The rooster pecked it to death and then devoured it in quick order. This was obviously not the first time the rooster had encountered such a spider.

* * * *

After a few months, while embarked on the cruiser *General Belgrano*, I was promoted to the rank of Lieutenant Commander. I asked for a new assignment as staff officer on a sea-going destroyer squadron staff. My request was promptly approved by Argentine authorities in Buenos Aires.

Before reporting to the destroyer squadron staff, Marlene and I took a wonderful month-long vacation. We went on a leisurely camping trip to the western part of Argentina in and around the Andes Mountains. Argentina is truly a place rich in food resources. I remember coming back to our tent with a stringer of nice trout caught from a pristine lake. My shoes were red from walking through wild strawberry fields. My favorite Greek sailor hat was filled full with the strawberries I picked near our campsite. Dinner fit for a king and his queen!

On this same trip, Marlene and I visited the pleasant town and ski resort of Bariloche in the Andes mountains. The architecture there would make you believe you were in Germany or Switzerland. About twelve percent of the Argentine population has a German last name and many of them live in and around Bariloche. In some villages in the Andes, German is spoken instead of Spanish. Bariloche is famous for chocolate, fondue, snow skiing and the beautiful huge lakes. While there we met with some Argentine friends one of whom Marlene coaxed onto an ice rink. As well, we happened to meet a U.S. Navy admiral and his family who were vacationing there.

Shortly after joining the destroyer squadron staff, a weapons officer on a destroyer assigned to the squadron became ill. I offered to assume his position on a Sumner class destroyer very similar to my first ship. The ship was an ex-U.S. Navy ship named ARA *Py*. Unlike my first ship, *Laffey*, this destroyer was equipped with a surface-to-surface (anti-ship) missile system known as Exocet. It was a European system. I devoted myself to reading technical manuals in an effort to figure out how to use it. To my way of thinking, the Argentine navy lacked a cohesive doctrine regarding how to use the system in company with other friendly ships that might unintentionally become targets of the missile. Once launched it had no means of recall or of self-destructing. So, I focused on exploring not only how best to deploy it but also how to defend against it. I submitted a detailed report to my superiors in the Argentine navy but I don't know if much came of it.

My most memorable event while assigned to ARA *Py* was in 1978 when we were at sea well off the coast of Argentina. We encountered a group of commercial Russian and Bulgarian fishing factory ships illegally operating inside the 200-mile limit of Argentine waters claimed as an Economic Enterprise Zone. The ships were larger trawler vessels equipped with scoop injection systems. That basically means large vacuum-like systems which sucked in huge amounts of krill. Krill are small shrimp common to the south Atlantic. They supposedly contain the highest protein per pound of any marine species in the ocean. Once they sucked up the krill, the factory ships would process them into blocks of livestock food. If you have ever been to Chile that's what they feed their chickens. Their eggs taste slightly fishy as a result.

I have forgotten exactly how many Russian and Bulgarian ships were in the group but it was probably four or five. I do remember a Bulgarian ship called *Sofia*. The lead Russian ship refused to acknowledge or respond to any communications whether by flashing light, signal flags or radio from my ship. They instead tried to run beyond the 200 nautical mile limit but we were in hot pursuit.

We kept our command authorities in Buenos Aires informed via radio communications. I was familiar with the Chief Naval Officer Authority in Buenos Aires. I knew him to be an aggressive no-

nonsense kind of person. I was not surprised when he issued a terse and brutal order to us which was "Sink them!" I was on the bridge of the ship with my Argentine Commanding Officer when this order was received. The only way this order could be executed was via me as the Weapons Officer. I knew what I had to do. The Commanding Officer was somewhat agitated by the order so I waited until the moment was right to tell him I should be relieved of my duties. I reminded him I was not an Argentine officer and if I, as a U.S. naval officer, were to fire upon a Russian ship it could evolve into a serious diplomatic incident. He looked at me with a rather blank look and then it sank in. I think he had forgotten I was a U.S. Navy officer. On one level, I was pleased I had assimilated so well and to the extent he had forgotten that. On another more important level, I did not wish to kill Russians or Bulgarians while serving under the flag of Argentina. He relieved me on the spot and I passed my duties to my gunnery assistant officer.

Things quickly got hot with the Bulgarian and Russian factory ships. My successor to the position of Weapons Officer, the Gunnery Officer, was ordered to fire on the lead Russian factory ship. Specifically, his orders were to fire as far forward on the ship as possible. In a marvel of naval gunnery, the first round to hit the ship took out a half moon shape from the stem of the ship. In other words, only half of the round hit the forward silhouette of the target ship. The impact must have been felt all over the Russian ship but still they failed to acknowledge any communications from us. They kept on steaming. The gunners on our ship kept on firing at the Russian ship. They gradually walked back the fire until about midships when the ship was disabled and went dead in the water. At that point, the Russians signaled one of their crew had lost a leg. They requested he be evacuated and treated on our ship, ARA *Py*.

The Russians and Bulgarians were relatively lucky. Every round fired upon them had been "blind loaded and plugged" meaning inert. The next rounds being readied in the loading trays were of the high explosive variety which would have had much more disastrous effect.

The gravely wounded Russian sailor along with a young Russian doctor were transferred by boat to our ship. Meanwhile, the other Russian and Bulgarian ships heaved to and were taken into custody at sea. All were herded into Puerto Madryn, the nearest Argentine port where they were interned pending diplomatic resolutions. The young Russian doctor was accorded the hospitality of the officer wardroom on my ship. I met him but had very little interaction with him. He seemed to have little time for niceties in any case. He was mostly interested in eating steak after steak. I gathered the Russian factory ships did not feed their people very well.

After taking the Russian and Bulgarian ships into Puerto Mardyn, my ship made sail north for our home port in Puerto Belgrano. I reassumed my position as weapons officer and everything became as before.

Shortly after we came back to our homeport in Puerto Belgrano, I was summoned to an interview with a young Argentine admiral named Jorge Isaac Anaya. Admiral Anaya was later to become the head of the Argentine navy and therefore one of the three junta members who ruled Argentina during the Falklands/Malvinas War. He was reportedly the driving force that propelled Argentina into that war. He wanted to talk to me about what I might tell U.S. authorities about what I had witnessed with respect to the interactions between the Argentine navy and the Russian and Bulgarian fishing ships. I gave him my account which was basically what I related to you above. I went on to tell him I had no intelligence taskings placed upon me by the U.S Navy. He wisely replied to the effect he believed me but the U.S. Naval Attaché in Buenos Aires and other intelligence authorities would no doubt be asking me questions and he wanted to know what I would tell them. This was my first but by no means my last interaction with Admiral Anaya. Importantly, it established some degree of mutual trust upon which we built a relationship that came into play later in important ways.

* * * *

In September of 1978, a group of three U.S. Navy surface ships (a frigate and two destroyers) and one U.S. Navy submarine, the

USS *Scamp* (SSN 588) arrived in the waters outside of the Argentine naval base of Puerto Belgrano. They were there as part of Exercise Unitas XIX. The Unitas exercises were a yearly joint event consisting of mostly anti-submarine exercises conducted by South American navies and units of the U.S. Navy.

The arrival of the U.S. Navy ships created a lot of activity on my part beginning with the assignment of harbor pilots to the arriving ships. I was particularly concerned about the U.S. submarine. As I recall, that submarine had a draft of 41 feet whereas the dredged channel leading to the naval base had a depth of only 44 feet. The commanding officer of the submarine declared he was unwilling to enter the port without a qualified pilot coming aboard fairly early and somewhat far at sea. Not only was the rather shallow depth of the channel a concern, there were also concerns centering on the submarine itself. Submarines are inherently less maneuverable on the surface compared to most surface ships. Plus, the submarine was nuclear powered. Any U.S. Navy ship touching the bottom is a serious concern but if a nuclear-powered vessel touches the bottom the consequences are amplified from a political standpoint.

Before the ships arrived, I reviewed the list of pilots assigned to them. I was gratified to learn the last name of the pilot assigned to the submarine was Murphy. I assumed Murphy would be able to communicate in English. Just before the ships arrived, I had occasion to meet Murphy who told me his grandfather, an immigrant from Ireland, had indeed been able to speak English, but Murphy himself did not.

Two senior U.S. Navy officers, one, the Naval Attaché serving in the U.S. Embassy in Buenos Aires, and the other serving in the Joint U.S. Military Group also in Buenos Aires, traveled to the Naval Base Puerto Belgrano to receive the U.S. Navy ships. I brought them up to speed on arrangements being made by the Argentine Navy including the piloting arrangements. I told them I was focusing on the submarine in particular. I informed them I intended to board the submarine with Murphy and act as his translator as he guided the submarine into the harbor. My fluency in nautical Spanish was considerably better than that of the more senior officers I was briefing and they approved of my plans.

I boarded an Argentine tugboat that went to sea at 2:00 AM with the pilots aboard in order to meet the U.S. Navy ships at a considerable distance off the shore of Argentina. We transferred pilots to the U.S. Navy surface ships and then approached the submarine. Personnel transfers at sea to submarines are considerably difficult especially when seas are choppy. Murphy and I embarked in a semi-rigid boat.

Murphy had a rather large butt. When our boat got close enough to the submarine, I gave him a hearty push and he managed to grab a rather flimsy rope ladder and he scrambled aboard. There was nobody to give me a push so I simply gave it my best effort which was not entirely successful. A wave swept me off the submarine and suddenly I was underwater looking up at the submarine. I swam up to the surface and grabbed the flimsy rope ladder while somehow managing to keep my hat. I climbed up inside the tower of the submarine and took station next to Murphy as he guided the submarine towards the harbor. A kind petty officer shoved a mug of hot coffee into my hands. I was soaked and shivering. I shook hands with the commanding officer who said something grateful about not having to fill out the paperwork that would have been necessarily required had I drowned.

The entry into the harbor was long and uncomfortably wet for me as I translated Murphy's rudder and speed orders. We arrived without incident. I went home to change my service dress blue uniform only to learn my other service dress blue uniform was at the local dry cleaners. A cocktail reception had been organized by the Argentine naval authorities to welcome the U.S. Navy officers. I attended in the same uniform but my wife periodically had to bring me wet towels to re-soak the fabric. If it was allowed to dry it showed unsightly white saltwater streaks.

I embarked Argentine ships during the exercises to observe and act as a liaison. A footnote to this story about Unitas XIX is this: the U.S. Navy ships left the Argentine naval base and proceeded to the Tierra Del Fuego city of Ushuaia which is the southernmost city in the world. A young sailor on one of the ships suffered a ruptured appendix and was sent to a local hospital. The city of Ushuaia lacked a U.S. consulate or other diplomatic support facilities. I was called upon for help. I flew to Ushuaia to lend help to the sailor who I recall as being very prone to crying. I arranged air transportation for him to get back to the U.S.A. I also remember giving him a good number of 3x5 cards annotated with both English and Spanish messages. Examples of such cards were explanations of his difficulties or "I have lost my passport or other identification papers." I recall learning he had eventually returned home and was returned to Navy service.

My last tasking while serving in the navy of Argentina in early 1978 was as navigator on their ice-breaker, ARA *General San Martín*. I am perhaps the only U.S. naval officer to have ever served in such a capacity. The U.S. Coast Guard, not the U.S. Navy, maintains command and control of all our United States fleet of ice-breakers. My entire time on the Argentine ice-breaker, I was in the Antarctic where we serviced and resupplied several Argentine bases there.

An ice-breaker is a very different kind of ship in basic ways. Unlike other ships, ice-breakers have no keels. It's built like a soup bowl and rides like one in rough seas which is the normal weather in the South Atlantic especially in the Drake Passage through which we often operated on our way to and from the Antarctic. The ship was powered by massive diesel engines. That ice-breaker was the worst riding ship I ever served on. The wardroom dining table was mounted on gimbals which received input from a stable element below decks. It would stay level no matter what the sea state was. Otherwise, one's potato would not stay on one's plate.

The Argentine flag officer embarked on the ice-breaker ARA

General San Martín was Admiral Jorge Anaya, whom I mentioned before. He sometimes invited me to have dinner with him in his cabin. We became socially closer and I think he began to trust me.

The ship was host to a number of notable people invited by the Argentine government; scientists, mining experts, etc. One of them was an ex-U.S. Navy Seal. He was a veteran of Vietnam as well as the Bay of Pigs operation. He was a Cuban exile living in Argentina after having married an Argentine woman. He had recently filmed an award-winning nature documentary, entitled *Había Una Vez en el Sur* in Spanish. In English, the film was known as *Killers of the Wild.* It was mostly about his study and documentation of whales in Argentina, particularly in the large Golfo Nuevo. He was the first person to film whales copulating in the wild. He became a celebrity in Argentina and was therefore invited to be on the ship. He came aboard with an assistant diver and a Zodiac type inflatable rigid boat.

Their interest was in studying leopard seals. Leopard seals are very large carnivores which eat mostly penguins and other seals. They have a large head about the size of that of a horse. The leopard seal is the Darth Vader character of nature in Antarctica. Once they climb onto a floating ice floe, the penguins and lesser seals around them would either flee or cower. The film crew would go down their blow holes in the ice and do ballsy things like punch them in the nose to assess their aggressiveness.

The ship also hosted some thirty or so husky sled dogs. They were imported to Argentina from Greenland as I recall. They were half wild. A number of them died from heat exhaustion in Buenos Aires before making it to Antarctica. The dogs were tied up on short leashes on the fantail of the ship. The short leashes were to prevent them from fighting with one another. The dogs thrived much better once they got to the colder weather south of the Antarctic Circle even though their fur was matted with icicles. We delivered the dogs to Argentine bases in the Antarctic where they were integrated into existing sled pulling teams. Ashore the dogs were not fed or otherwise provisioned nor were they given shelter. They dug holes into the snow for their shelter. When it was time to feed, the lead sled dog would simply stop. The dogs were released to kill penguins or seals. The dogs rolled in the blood and offal of their kills and then got back into their harnesses.

Once we arrived in Antarctic waters, my job as navigator became more and more complicated. Navigating a ship in the Antarctic can be very difficult. First of all, a navigator could rarely rely on celestial star sightings taken with a sextant. The sky was typically overcast and stars could not be seen. Second, LORAN coverage was spotty and very unreliable. Third, our compass got sloppier the closer we got to the South Pole.

Imagine, if you will, being at the South Pole. Every direction you could point to would be north. The closer we got to the South Pole the less accurate our compass became. My most reliable navigation tool was the fathometer, which measured depth under the ship. I would take a sounding and then compare it to the charts which showed depths. I would make educated guesses about where we were. Once we approached visible landmarks, such as mountains, I could firmly fix our position but otherwise it involved a lot of guesswork.

Ice-breaking was an interesting endeavor. Not all ice is equal. The ship was equipped with a masthead-mounted zoom camera we used to assess the type of ice we intended to break. Blue ice was the worst. Blue ice could be a thousand years old and tougher than steel. We used the zoom camera to pick paths through the most breakable ice which was generally lighter in color. Our paths through the ice packs were only rarely straight lines. The ship did not generally ram the ice to break it. Instead, we would ride up on the ice and allow the soup-bowl configuration of our hull to crush it. Then we would back and fill to create a path through which the ship could proceed.

Obviously, the Antarctic is a stark and unforgiving environment. No matter if I were at sea or walking around ashore, I always felt we were only one accident or mechanical failure away from disaster. For example, the ship relied upon two powerful diesel-electric engines. We needed both to break the ice. If we lost one, the ship would end up frozen into the ice pack.

I was told and I believed a story that had the ARA *General San Martín* losing an engine while in the ice pack some time before my presence on her. According to the story, the faulty engine was repaired but not before colder weather set in. An Argentine air force C-130 logistic aircraft landed on the ice near the ship. The aircraft brought provisions to the ship and then evacuated most of the crew leaving only a skeleton crew aboard for most of a year until seasonal conditions allowed the ship to break out again.

Our main mission in the Antarctic was to resupply several Argentine Antarctic bases. During the winter months the thick ice, which could extend sixty miles or so from the coastal bases, was unbreakable. During the summer months (January plus or minus) we could manage to reach the bases by breaking through the reduced ice packs.

I remember one of my first times ashore in the Antarctic when we resupplied a smaller Argentine army base. The outpost had lost its heating system during a long, long winter. We were very well received because we were bringing them a circuit board which would restore operation to their solid-state heating system. The people who manned the post had been relying on a kitchen range as their only source of heat for some months. They would huddle around the range eating directly from frying pans while getting warm. They could not eat at the tables because their food would freeze to the plates quickly. None of them had changed clothes for a long time for the same reason.

At that same base, I remember walking around exploring a huge nearby colony of Emperor penguins. The colony consisted of thousands of the birds. The smell was awful because so many dead penguins were underfoot. Those dead penguins were seasonally thawing out and off-gassing after having died a long time ago.

Likewise, the base dump was temporarily thawing and giving off noxious odors.

The penguins were hilarious in that they surged toward me in mass because they were curious. Penguins apparently have poor eyesight. Once they got close enough to see me, they became scared and retreated only to quickly become curious again. The mass of them around me constantly surged toward me then away from me.

Upon occasion, we would give the crew a break from the constant rolling and tossing of the ship and allow the ship to freeze into the ice overnight thereby stabilizing it. Argentines being Argentines, could not go too long without having an *asado*. With the ship stabilized, they would build a fire on the ice and roast short ribs and other types of meat. There's nothing like enjoying a big *asado* washed down with good Argentine wine on the ice on a sunny day in the Antarctic.

The Argentines have long sought to reinforce their territorial claims in the Antarctic. They have done things like issuing postal stamps from there. When I went ashore to one of their bases, I met a young mother who was the wife of an Argentine Army officer. I think she and her husband were selected to be posted there because she was pregnant. Her baby was the first baby ever born in the Antarctic. I was asked to hold her baby in my arms for a photo opportunity. I acquiesced even though I knew I might be being set up. By that time, I felt like I was to some degree becoming Argentine. The photo of me, a North American naval officer, holding the first ever Argentine baby born in the Antarctic, may have been featured in the primary newspaper of Argentina, *El País*.

* * * *

My tour as an exchange officer with the navy of Argentina was coming to an end. I found it difficult to communicate with my detailer at the Washington-based Bureau of Personnel except by written snail mail. The detailer was the person who held my fate in his hands as regards my next assignment. Detailers are basically flesh merchants. This was in 1979 before electronic communication via e-mail came to be. I requested to be assigned as an executive officer (second in command) on a U.S. Navy destroyer. My aim was to subsequently be approved for command of a destroyer.

The needs of the Navy once again re-asserted themselves. I received orders to be the missile officer of USS *Long Beach* (CGN-9) based in San Diego. I was somewhat disappointed with the assignment but I regarded USS *Long Beach* to be the preeminent missile cruiser in the U.S. Navy. I took that as consolation.

A KENTUCKY BOY GOES TO SEA AS A NAVAL OFFICER

CHAPTER 9

Duty on USS *Long Beach* (CGN-9) and My Subsequent Assignment to the U.S. Navy War College

Returning to the States and following some leave with family in Connecticut and Florida, my wife and I moved to modest but pleasant Navy housing across the bay from San Diego to Coronado Naval Air Station on Coronado Island. I reported aboard USS *Long Beach* (CGN-9) which was berthed at Coronado. I could walk to work. The *Long Beach* was a large nuclear-powered cruiser with about 1,200 souls aboard. She was powered with two large nuclear reactors which could have supplied a medium sized U.S. city in terms of energy demands.

As Missile Officer, I was in charge of a formidable missile battery of SM-2 Standard Missiles mostly designed for area air-defense but also capable of anti-ship applications. I had more than eighty people reporting to me. During my tour I had occasion to shoot a number of my missiles at drone targets all of which hit their targets. As a matter of fact, I never missed the target drone including earlier when I was weapons officer on USS *Schofield*.

Given my relatively senior status, I was not required to stand watches driving the ship. I regarded that as a real luxury. I got more sleep than I was used to heretofore in the U.S. Navy. Shortly after I reported aboard, the ship deployed for eight months to the Western Pacific. I left Marlene on Coronado, pregnant with our first child.

A touching event occurred when I was on the *Long Beach*. One day I was standing watch as Command Duty Officer when the messenger of the quarter deck watch came to me to inform me a Chief Boatswains Mate had approached the quarter-deck inquiring about me. I came down to the quarterdeck and met the Chief who was in a dress uniform. I recognized him right away. He had worked for me on USS *Schofield* when he was a First-Class Boatswain Mate. He was a wonderful sailor but he was at the time having severe marital problems. He began to go on unauthorized absences. I took a special interest in him. One day, I went to his Navy assigned housing quarters unannounced in an effort to find him and persuade him to report for duty.

He was not there but his toxic but rather attractive wife was. She put moves on me probably thinking it was another good way to hurt and damage her husband. She also gave me a black powder handgun saying she feared her husband. I took the handgun but left her alone. I later told this sailor of his wife's behavior. Meanwhile, my commanding officer busted him to a lower pay-grade not once but twice. He went from a First-Class Boatswain Mate to a Third-Class Boatswain Mate.

I got on the telephone with the Navy Personnel Bureau. I effectively communicated my high esteem for the sailor and my low esteem for his wife. I recommended he be assigned to a new afloat command somewhere away from San Diego where he could get a new start. I correctly guessed his wife would not follow him. They divorced and he went on to a new ship. He thrived in a new command where other officers came to share my high opinion of him.

USS *Long Beach* (CGN-9), my last U.S. Navy ship

In time, he made the rank of Chief Petty Officer (E-7) and secured a good Navy career. By some means, he managed to keep track of me. His purpose in visiting me on Long Beach was to thank me for my support and faith in him. I was moved by his gesture.

While at sea, I took a Strategy and Policy correspondence course from the U.S. Naval War College. I studied in detail historical subjects like the ancient Peloponnesian Wars between Sparta and Athens. The emphasis there was upon the advantages and difficulties of alliances. Subsequently, I studied things like the concept of limited warfare as embodied by Bismarck and the unification of Germany. I studied Lord Nelson. During my cruise, I completed about one third of the U.S. Naval War College Command and Staff course. That came in very handy later when I was sent to the War College after my tour on *Long Beach.*

Meanwhile, Marlene and another officer's wife planned a trip based upon our deployment itinerary. She met me in the Philippines and Hong Kong. Although I was very busy, we did find time to snorkel off Grande Island in Subic Bay, enjoy dinners of Mahi Mahi in the Subic Officer's Club and sample dim sum in Hong Kong. Our daughter Katie made the trip as well. Marlene was three months pregnant at the time so Katie never saw any of it.

Before the ship was deployed to the Western Pacific a young ensign reported aboard. He took over a division of technicians associated with my missile battery. He was a tall, gangly and pale-looking individual. He was also a strange bird with what later proved to be suicidal tendencies. While we were in port at San Diego, a California State Highway Patrol officer came aboard asking to meet with me. The trooper told me the ensign had purchased a handgun from a San Diego gun store. I did not regard that as illegal but the trooper went on to say the gun store owner had a bad feeling about the ensign and thought he may have purchased the handgun with a possible intention to use it on himself. I promised to talk to the ensign which I did forthwith. The ensign denied the gun store owner's allegation. Again, I felt something was very wrong with the ensign. The young officer and I decided to talk to him on a more frequent basis. Eventually, he told me he had sold the handgun back to the gun store. I called the gun store and was told the ensign had indeed returned the firearm. My suspicions about his mental state remained.

When the ship visited a South Korean port, the ensign visited a pharmacy there. South Korean drugstores are not constrained by controls common to the U.S. They can and do sell a lot of drugs over the counter for which a prescription would be required in this country. The ensign bought a goodly amount of what were likely powerful barbiturates.

Upon returning to sea, the ensign failed to wake up for a midwatch and could not be roused. USS Long Beach had an assigned medical doctor aboard. The doctor was summoned to the ensign's bunk where he determined the ensign was alive but comatose. I watched the doctor administer dose after dose of Narcan to the ensign. Narcan is a powerful narcotic-cancelling drug. Usually, one dose is sufficient to cancel any overdose. The ship was still close to South Korea and returned there where we effected a boat transfer of the ensign to a U.S. medical facility. I am not sure what became of the ensign but he was not returned to the *Long Beach*. I suspect he may have suffered serious brain damage leading to his discharge from the Navy.

When my deployment ended, I returned to San Diego. Marlene was eight months pregnant by then. There's an old adage in the Navy: you have to be there for the keel laying but you might not be there for the launching. Luckily, in the case of my daughter, Katie, I was present for both events.

USS *Long Beach* was sent to the Bremerton Naval Shipyard in Washington State for an extended overhaul and modernization including a significant command and control upgrade called Aegis: a state-of-the-art computerized system. We found a house to rent in Bremerton. I was promoted to the rank of full Commander. Shortly thereafter my second daughter Audrey was born in 1981.

Another significant thing happened to me while I was embarked on *Long Beach*. Toward the end of my tour in 1982, the Falklands/Malvinas War broke out. The shuttle diplomacy of U.S. General Alexander Haig and Henry Kissinger broke down to the point where Argentine authorities were basically left with very diminished communication channels with U.S. authorities. One night when I was standing a Command Duty Officer watch on USS *Long Beach*, my wife called me saying my old friend Carlos had called my home telephone number with an urgent request I call him back.

By this point in time, Admiral Anaya had become one of the three junta members ruling Argentina and Carlos was his principal aide. Both Admiral Anaya and Carlos had been close associates of mine. I called Carlos right away from a telephone on USS *Long Beach*. He basically told me Argentine naval air assets had just sunk the HMS *Antrim*, a Royal Navy frigate. Further, he said he and Admiral Anaya did not think the British were being honest with us in terms of how badly the Argentines were hurting the Royal Navy. He asked me to quickly get this information into U.S. Navy intelligence channels.

The next morning, I sought out the nearest intelligence officer I could find who happened to be on a nearby ship in Bremerton, Washington. Next, I called an old Navy friend who occupied an intelligence position on the Joint Command Staff (JCS) in the Pentagon. Turns out Carlos was right. This was the first news we had of this ship sinking.

I had suddenly become an Argentine intelligence agent. Carlos was my controller. We began to talk on at least a daily basis. My old friend at JCS then handed me off to another conduit for communications. Admiral Anaya later died of a heart attack he suffered while being questioned by Argentine authorities about his role during the "Dirty War" before the Falklands/Malvinas War.

During that time I was dealing with the U.S. Navy Personnel Command regarding my next assignment. As I became more senior (I was now a Commander) my dealings with the Personnel Command seemed to become more difficult and acrimonious. I had asked to be assigned to the Naval War College in as much as I had already completed about one third of the curriculum by correspondence. I was told I would instead be sent to the U.S. Marine Corps War College. I protested and requested a Flag Officer Review before such orders were written. Gratefully, the Flag Officer who reviewed my request agreed with me. I received orders to detach from *Long Beach* and report to the U.S. Naval War College in Newport, Rhode Island, as a student in the Command and Staff College.

Because I was getting frequent intelligence updates from Carlos, I was told my orders to the War College might have to be delayed or cancelled until after the Falklands/Malvinas War ended. I did not like that. I told the Bureau of Personnel I could easily call Carlos as I traveled across country on my way to Newport, Rhode Island, by simply calling him from pay phones. Then I could feed information via a secure phone line to my U.S. Navy intelligence contacts. They did not like that but they relented and I proceeded to once again drive my car across the country. I had hoped they realized it was my show and not theirs. As stated earlier, my dealings with the Navy Personnel Command were becoming more acidic.

As the war turned more and more against Argentina, Carlos's information became more like disinformation. I remember him telling me Argentine forces were preparing to conduct an armored counterattack against British forces which had by that time come ashore on the main island. I knew Argentina had no armored forces on the islands. I just forwarded the raw information knowing it was bogus and also knowing it would be perceived as such in the Pentagon.

By the time I arrived at the War College in Newport the war was over. The Secretary of the Navy, John Lehman, had ordered a War College Study focusing on the War. Because I had already completed a third of the curriculum by correspondence, I was drafted into the Falklands/Malvinas War study team operating within the Center for Advanced Research at the War College. My job was to be a surrogate Argentine officer looking at the war from the Argentine perspective.

I was given extraordinary access to British naval authorities such as Admiral Sandy Woodward (the officer in tactical command of Royal Navy forces during the War) as well as to the most senior Argentine authorities like Admiral Anaya to whom I already had access. To make a long story shorter, I authored a policy piece entitled "Argentine Policy Motivations During the Falklands War and the Aftermath." It was published in the U.S. Naval War College Review in 1983. It linked a number of geopolitical considerations to Argentine policy motivations: the fact that if Argentina had gained the islands Argentina would then have the largest territorial sea in the world. These waters are rich in oil resources in the sea bed as well as substantial fisheries. Had Argentina prevailed during the war, the country could have logically and eventually joined OPEC (Organization of the Petroleum Exporting Countries). Further, such a territorial sea would strengthen Argentina's Antarctic claims while at the same time weakening the British position in the Antarctic at a time when the Antarctic treaty was set to expire. With British

Graduation from the Naval War
College in 1983 with my daughters
Katie and Audrey in attendance

influence severely weakened, Argentina and Chile could more easily come to terms regarding their long-standing territorial claims in the Antarctic. Both Argentina and Chile base their claims in the Antarctic on the geography of the Andes Mountains. Their common border is based on the Andes and the Andes Mountains submerge in the South Atlantic but reappear above the sea in the Antarctic.

My policy piece was academically well received and has been referenced a number of times by other researchers and particularly by authorities in Argentina. As I will describe later, I was awarded Argentina's highest formal diplomatic recognition in connection with my writing.

I continued with and completed the rest of my studies at the Naval War College. Those studies included a lot of sophisticated and interesting war gaming plus a course called "Non-Quantitative Factors in Government Administration." This interesting course was aimed at preparing us for major staff duty. Most of us War College graduates would be assigned to staff duty in Washington, D.C., probably in the Pentagon. The course focused on several case studies involving major acquisitions, but it was basically aimed at how to navigate within and around huge bureaucracies. I was given orders to report in for a job on the Chief of Naval Operations Staff in the Pentagon. I found the course very useful in preparing me for that job.

At the same time, I managed to pick up a master's degree in international affairs from Salve Regina University in Newport, Rhode Island.

A KENTUCKY BOY GOES TO SEA AS A NAVAL OFFICER

CHAPTER 10

Duty in Washington, D.C.

My family and I moved to Springfield, Virginia, not far from the Washington, D.C. Beltway. We bought a townhouse and my young family moved in. I reported for duty on the Chief of Naval Operations Staff in Washington, D.C., in 1983. My position was as an action officer in OP-63 (Foreign Military Sales) which is within the OP-06 Plans and Policy Division. To my chagrin, I would be working for my old nemesis who had been my commanding officer on *Schofield*. He had by that time been promoted to Rear Admiral.

This time things were different. Instead of terrorizing me, he regarded me as a known quantity already trained to his expectations. He gave me a surprisingly long leash and he gave me good fitness reports. It might have also helped that I was now fluent in Spanish and he needed someone like me to oversee the huge foreign military sales program with Spain as that country was just entering NATO.

The Spanish program I oversaw amounted to $3 billion dollars in active volume. It consisted of ship building programs, multiple major aircraft acquisition programs (F-18 and Harrier Jump-Jets) and a myriad of lesser but important acquisitions. It was a complicated task for me which required a lot of contact with the Spanish embassy in Washington, D.C., as well as with various U.S. Navy technical systems commands. I frequently hosted meetings in the D.C. area with Spanish military authorities so as to update them on various issues. Almost all of the Spaniards smoked but smoking was increasingly banned in and around our meeting venues. When hosting meetings with the Spanish, I always took care to surreptitiously produce ash trays from a stash in the desk of my office. I also traveled to Spain fairly frequently on business connected to my stewardship of their acquisition programs.

For some reason, I was also charged with responsibility for all Navy foreign military sales to Yugoslavia. That was a much smaller program but it was interesting for reasons I will relate later.

Typically, my duties involved writing point papers which were informational or which required decisions by flag officers. For the latter kind of point paper, I would run those papers around the Pentagon in an effort to gain approval from seven or so admirals or high-level civil servants. Seven admirals have never agreed on anything but I quickly learned if I could get the bean counters (accountants) and lawyers on my side about half the battle was won. Then, if the Chief of Naval Operations agreed with the position set forth in the point paper the decision was more or less assured. Point papers had to be very concise. Most admirals will not read anything over two pages long.

A good example of what I did was oversee the sale of the AN/SQR-19 Towed Array Sonar System to Spain. This system was state-of-the art and very sophisticated. It had never been sold to any foreign country. The sale was complicated by politics at the U.S. congressional level. A somewhat older and less sophisticated system, the SQR-18 was being built in Long Island. In an effort to throw business to Long Island, the congressman from that congressional district attached a rider to the defense authorization bill in an effort to kill the sale of the SQR-19 system to Spain. The U.S. Navy submariners were also against the sale because it would optimize the Spanish Navy's ability to detect and track U.S. submarines.

Luckily, the Chief of Naval Operations, who tended to center on issues having to do with alliances was in favor of the sale. It might not have mattered but I knew the Chief of Naval Operations who at the time was Admiral J.D. Watkins. He had been Commander of my flotilla when I was aboard USS *Schofield*. In the end, the sale proceeded. We essentially wore down the opposition. The congressman agreed to withdraw his rider from the defense appropriation bill and the submariners got in line with the Chief of Naval Operations. I spent a lot of shoe leather running around briefing various officials. I remember one such official being then-Congressman John McCain.

Not long after I arrived in Washington, the Argentine Ambassador summoned me to the Argentine Embassy. I was unsure about why he wanted to see me but I was glad to comply. The ambassador sat me down for coffee with several of his staff. He announced the reason for my presence: He was to induct me into *El Orden del Libertador General San Martín* (The Order of the Liberator General San Martín) in recognition of my having published the piece I had written at the Naval War College: "Argentine Policy Motivations During the Falklands War and the Aftermath." That article had been very well received in Argentina. After our coffee he awarded me my certificate of membership in the Order.

This honor was the highest diplomatic award conferred by the Government of Argentina upon foreign political officials and foreign military. Their General San Martín was analogous to our General George Washington. I was quite surprised, impressed and honored. Unfortunately, my certificate of membership was lost during a subsequent move. I have written to the Argentine Ambassador in Washington, D.C., in an effort to substantiate my claim but he has not responded at the time I am writing this. You'll have to take my word for it.

As mentioned, I was also placed in charge of all U.S. Navy foreign military sales to Yugoslavia which was a communist country. Many or most requests from Yugoslavia did not get fulfilled. They would ask us to sell them, for example, one Harpoon missile which is a sophisticated anti-ship missile. It was pretty clear they wanted it to tear apart and then reverse engineer it. Or perhaps they might give it to the Russians who would do the same thing. We would politely decline such requests. The Yugoslavians also asked to buy our Mark 46 acoustic homing torpedoes. We pointed out such torpedoes were for open ocean, deep water scenarios. We asked them to consider the Mark 44 torpedo which was more suitable for their shallow Adriatic Sea. They refused the offer.

I was asked/ordered to accompany Ronald Lauder, Assistant Secretary of Defense as part of his entourage for a high-level visit to Yugoslavia. Ronald Lauder, the son of Estée Lauder of cosmetics fame, was a substantial donor to the Republican Party and had previously served as U.S. Ambassador to Yugoslavia.

Upon arrival in Belgrade, I was informed my luggage had been lost. The same thing had happened when I had visited there before. I strongly suspected Yugoslavian security authorities were going through my luggage looking for who knows what. For two days, I wore the clothing I had worn when flying there. I washed my underwear in the bathroom sink of my hotel room and hung it on the balcony outside my room to dry. A gust of wind blew my underwear onto the roof of an adjacent building. I wondered if the security people thought I had made some kind of dead drop. I imagined them waiting for someone to pick up my underwear to retrieve a secret message hidden in microdots of the elastic. I went free and easy for a day and then my luggage finally showed up.

When I went to the hotel bar a younger Yugoslavian gentleman took a bar stool next to mine. He sipped Coca Cola. He was my tail. If I went to the bathroom, so did he. He was not subtle.

Our meetings went on for several days in Belgrade with a number of military and civilian dignitaries. The subjects related mostly to defense cooperation. Dinners were lavish eight course affairs washed down with ample quantities of slivovitz: a potent plum brandy. We even drank the fiery slivovitz with breakfast.

We also went to Sarajevo to tour a Bosnian factory that manu-
factured armored personnel carriers for their army. About half the
workers were Muslim. Islam had been introduced some centuries
before when the Turks invaded the Balkans. The Yugoslavian
Muslims I observed seemed to be low key. From what I could tell,
the Muslims and the Christians got along well. There were no obvious hints of the coming ethnic cleansing which brought thousands
of deaths, the coming brutal war nor the breakup of Yugoslavia.

A KENTUCKY BOY GOES TO SEA AS A NAVAL OFFICER

CHAPTER 11

Naval Attaché Duty in Spain

T owards the end of my rather successful tour in Washington, D.C., I was made aware of a job I wanted. It was that of a naval attaché in the U.S. Embassy in Madrid. The timing was perfect in that the job was coming open when I was slated to leave my job in the Pentagon. I was fluent in Spanish. Further, I had lots of professional contacts and experience in Spain. So, I applied for the job.

One problem among many with the Bureau of Naval Personnel is that of selective hearing. When I asked to be assigned as an attaché in Spain the bureau took that to mean I was simply willing to be assigned overseas. The bureau always has a number of difficult postings to fill overseas and they were more than willing to pound round pegs into square holes to do so. When I called the bureau to ask about my upcoming orders, my detailer told me they were working on orders to send me to either Madagascar or Pakistan. They mentioned my wife and I would enjoy riding horses on the beach in the morning in Pakistan. My relations with the Bureau of Naval Personnel seemed to be going from acidic to toxic. I decided to take matters into my own hands. I was worried they would cut orders. Once orders were cut and delivered, I would have to execute those orders. I happened to have an upcoming business trip to Spain scheduled.

While in Spain, I stopped in the U.S. Embassy and asked to speak with the U.S. Ambassador whom I had met several times and with whom I felt some mutual affinity. I told him I would like to join his diplomatic team as an attaché. He immediately agreed to same. I asked him to request me by name via State Department Channels. That's how I got the job. I knew at the time I was committing potential career suicide by going outside of Navy channels but I frankly did not care. I just wanted a job I knew I would be very good at.

Upon return to Washington, D.C., the bureau called me. They were not amused at all, but ambassadors tend to get what they ask for and, in this case, it was me. My orders to report as an attaché were cut. I was warned I could not expect much warmth from the bureau in terms of future postings down the road. I had committed the cardinal sin of going outside of Navy channels to secure a job. I called it initiative but they called it something more akin to insubordination. Still, I got what I wanted.

A military attaché is a diplomatic-level posting via the Defense Intelligence Agency (DIA). My wife and I reported into the 3 month DIA course for attaché training in Washington, D.C. The training was excellent and interesting but perhaps a bit spookier than we would need in a rather friendly and allied country like Spain. Still, we absorbed it all including being instructed how to shoot a handgun left-handed. This was to allow better shooting from a motor vehicle.

Following the DIA training, I arrived with my family in Madrid. We stayed at a hotel for a few weeks and then rented a nice house to the west of Madrid. My daughters were both starting elementary school at that time. We had the option of enrolling my girls in an American school in Madrid but my wife and I agreed upon enrolling them in a private Spanish Catholic school not too far from our house. We were a bit worried about that because my daughters spoke no Spanish and their school had no English-speaking staff. We should not have worried. They started school in September. By Christmas they were basically fluent in Spanish.

Some practices and cultural rituals we parents did not understand well at first. One was *disfraz*, which to the Spanish means "fancy dress" or "costume." Some days the Spanish school would designate as *disfraz*, meaning the girls were supposed to dress in *Sevillana* dresses which all Spanish girls seemed to own in as much as every young Spanish girl knows how to perform the expressive *Sevillana* dance. When we received a notice from the school, we thought *disfraz* meant disguise as in Halloween costumes. So, we dressed my youngest daughter in a Snoopy costume for her *disfraz* day. In spite of the gaffe, it was kind of a hit in terms of being a fashion statement. It certainly attracted attention. Now that we knew what *disfraz* meant, we purchased *Sevillana* dresses for both our daughters. Both daughters learned to dance the *Sevillana*.

Upon occasion, my wife and I would meet the parents of our daughters' classmates. Those parents were very surprised we were Americans. Our daughters acted and spoke like typical Spanish kids. To this day they speak good Spanish and maintain friendships with a number of their classmates. Also, to this day, one of my daughter's young friends calls me her American father. She has visited us in the U.S. and I regard her as my Spanish daughter. I am very glad we immersed my girls in Spanish language and culture early on.

As mentioned, as an attaché I was diplomatically accredited. I was accredited directly to the King of Spain, Juan Carlos I de Borbón, in as much as he was the Commander in Chief of Spanish Armed Forces. Other diplomats in the American embassy were accredited to Spanish political authorities. They salivated at the level of access we military attachés had with the King and his Queen Sofia.

Since we were accredited to the King, we had a formal audience once a year with the King and Queen at their royal palace, but we saw them more frequently than that on the busy diplomatic cocktail circuit. Both the King and Queen got to know me on a first name basis although we never addressed them by anything other than *Su*

Majestad (Your Majesty). On the other hand, the King got to know me well enough to occasionally ask me to tell him dirty jokes which he seemed to enjoy.

From the start, I was very much impressed with both the King and Queen. Both speak several languages fluently. They were skilled at talking to mixed language groups as was the foreign attaché group we were part of without leaving anyone out of the conversation,

I remember the Queen telling me how much she and the King had enjoyed their honeymoon in the States shortly after their marriage in the early sixties. She specifically mentioned her memory of being hosted at a dinner with the Navy Midshipmen at the U.S. Naval Academy in Annapolis, Maryland. Suddenly, I recalled her son Prince Felipe was at that moment visiting in the U.S. and furthermore that he was in Maryland not far from the U.S. Naval Academy. Further, Prince Felipe was currently a midshipman in the Spanish Navy. He is now the current King of Spain. That evening before going home, I stopped at the embassy where I drafted a cable to the Chief of Naval Operations, the U.S. State Department and the Commandant of the Naval Academy among others. In my cable, I recounted my conversation with the Queen and the fact that Prince Felipe was then visiting in Maryland. I asked for an invitation to be extended to the Prince for a dinner with the midshipmen at the Naval Academy. The invitation was quickly extended and accepted by the Prince.

Some months later, my wife and I were attending a social event where the King and Queen were in attendance. The Queen noticed me and walked across the room to me. She very graciously and sincerely thanked me for making her son's visit to the Naval Academy happen. This was typical of both the King and Queen. They both have extremely busy schedules but they remember small details like my conversation with the Queen and how the invitation to her son unfolded. The Queen knew I had made it happen. I was impressed by her attention to such things.

Me having an audience with the King of Spain

By way of background, the King averted an attempted military coup by the Spanish military in 1981 after the death of El Caudillo General Franco. The King did this on the basis of his personal character and his gravitas. This gained for him immense public support and affection from the Spanish people at large. Of late, he has suffered some public relations disasters in terms of potential scandal but I hope he will be remembered in the terms I remember him. He was the authority who stewarded in the new Spain and brought it into NATO.

An anecdote: One late night my wife and I were returning home from a social event in Madrid. I paused at a stop light and under a bright street light. A motorcyclist pulled up alongside. The rider was wearing a helmet with a dark visor. He looked at us. Then he raised his visor and smiled at us. He had recognized us. The King liked to drive around Madrid at night on his motorcycle. He enjoyed the brief anonymity it afforded him.

My daily routine as an attaché was always busy. At that time, the U.S. Navy had about 300 ship visits to Spain every year. It was my responsibility to gain diplomatic clearance for each and every ship visit on an individual basis. The conventional ships were easy. The nuclear-powered ships presented a bit more of a challenge. Spanish authorities had some sort of formula governing approval of nuclear-powered vessel visits. The formula probably relied on politics and visibility. For example, Rota, Spain, was easier to get nuclear power ship visit clearance simply because it was more remote from large population centers. We had only two naval attachés on station (one was my senior as well as the Defense Attaché and therefore the head of our group). Obviously, we could not meet every U.S. Navy ship visiting Spain. There were simply too many. Instead, we relied upon a network of ship husbanding agents and consular agents in several Spanish ports to do that for us. Nevertheless, if the U.S. Navy ship had an Admiral embarked, we (usually me) would meet the ship (usually an aircraft carrier). We would arrange protocol visits on behalf of the Admiral to local authorities, accompany him on those visits, act as a translator and generally assist in any fashion needed. Needless to say, I traveled a lot within Spain.

Our social agenda was always hectic. We were constantly on the move to cocktail parties and dinners. I recorded 24 separate social events within the month of one December. Luckily, I have a hollow leg and can hold my booze well.

The DIA required us to entertain foreign guests in our home at least twice a month. I always looked forward to inviting the Argentine naval attaché and his wife to my home. I knew him from my service in Argentina. He was an old friend. Usually, I would invite the British Royal Navy attaché and his wife (who was native Argentine) to the same dinner but I was careful not to overtly tell either of them this because technically their countries were still at war after the Falklands affair. The Argentines and the British attachés were prohibited from actively socializing but could do so if they happened to meet on the cocktail circuit. That is where I came in as a facilitator.

The British and Argentine attachés had a lot of state-to-state business to talk about and in effect they established a kind of back channel over coffee, brandy and cigars in my dining room. They appreciated me and my willingness to be an intermediary. I appreciated them, too. I reported everything I heard in my intelligence reporting. They knew that but they were willing to accept it as a cost of doing business.

My wife and I typically had two or three Thanksgiving dinners in our home each November because they were so popular with our foreign friends. We could not host all who wished to come so we would repeat the event. They loved the turkey, the stuffing and other associated side dishes but most did not like the pumpkin pie. I guess that was too American for their taste. For my part, I valued invitations from my Portuguese counterparts around the Christmas holidays. They always served bacalao which is a seasonal Portuguese cod dish I love.

The life of an attaché brought daily surprises. You never knew who might walk through the door to the embassy. Once it was a senior Iranian navy officer seeking to defect. He came to the front desk in the embassy and asked the marine security guard to speak to a U.S. Navy officer. He ended up in front of my desk. He explained he had fled to Spain and that a death squad was on his tail. He asked me for asylum in the U.S. I conducted an initial interview and then turned him over to the CIA people in the embassy. They quickly put him on an airplane bound for the U.S. Then I realized my wife was booked on the same flight on a trip to visit her family. There was little I could do beyond telling my wife. She was not happy but all came out well. Their airplane arrived without incident.

My wife, Marlene, was selected for a position at the embassy. She was hired as the Community Liaison Officer which entailed being the contact person between the embassy and the American

My wife, Marlene, and I
attending a formal affair

community the embassy served in and around Madrid. It was a de-
manding and challenging job which she handled well. She reported
directly to the deputy chief of mission.

Given our very busy work and social schedule, we found it necessary to hire a full-time, live-in maid and nanny for our children.
She was a delightful, young Filipino woman named Zenny. She
made our life much easier. I now very much regret having lost
contact with her over the years. We still consider her to be family.

At first, I wondered how to go about gaining foreign intelligence contacts. It turned out they often sought me out. Various dignitaries and military authorities knew I was a declared, overt intelligence operative and many wanted some way to make intelligence inputs of various kinds into the U.S. system. At the time, the Iran-Iraq War was happening. I was at a cocktail party in Madrid and found myself talking to an Iraqi official. He gave me a tidbit of information about the war and I reported it. This happened a lot. Often, I did not know if the information was valid or valuable but I reported it anyway knowing it would be sorted out by the intelligence analysts. Typically, I would code my sources to protect them.

I also was a de facto member of the "Blue Mafia." The Blue Mafia was the nickname for a rather informal group comprised of all naval attachés from countries diplomatically represented in Madrid. We met socially once a month in one of our homes. The smaller group of NATO naval attachés also met frequently for lunch. We typically shared a lot of intelligence germane to NATO.

While stationed in Madrid, I became an aficionado of bullfighting. At first, I did not understand bullfighting very well. I mentioned that to a Spanish naval officer friend who told me I needed to go to a bullfight with a Spaniard who would explain the finer points to me. He then served in such a capacity himself. One of the first things he told me was to watch the matador's feet above all. He said a good matador moved his feet hardly at all during the fight. Instead, he moved the bull with good cape work. He also explained that a bullfight is not a sport but rather a spectacle.

There are three phases for each bullfight, called *tercios* (thirds). Each phase is signaled by different music played by a band in the arena. In the first phase, the bull and the matador basically size up one another. The matador uses a larger red cape to cause the bull to make passes. Both the matador and the crowd of fans observe the bull carefully. One thing they observe is whether the bull focuses upon the matador himself or the upon the cape. Any bull that focuses upon the matador is suspect and is often quickly rejected by both the matador as well as a booing crowd of fans.

Young Spanish males, who fancy themselves aspiring matadors, often cannot resist giving young bulls in the fields a few passes with something that to them resembles a cape. The bull rather quickly learns to focus on the difference between a cape and the person wielding same. The bull that reflexively focuses on the matador is then considered ruined in terms of bullfighting.

In the second phase of the bullfight, the matador stands back and watches as the *bandilleros* and *picadors* who are mounted on horses with one eye of the horse effectively masked, take turns sticking colorful *bandilleros* and spear-like implements into the hump of the bull. Their objective is to loosen up the shoulder muscles of the bull so as to both enrage the bull and get the horns lower in advance of the third and final phase of the fight.

In the final phase, the matador takes center stage in the arena with a smaller cape called a *muleta* and a smallish sword called a *vara*. The matador gives the bull a number of passes while continuing to observe and assess the bull and to demonstrate his mastery of the bull's movements. At the end of the fight, the matador goes over the head of the charging bull with the sword as he aims at a point about the size of a quarter between the shoulders. If the matador's nerve holds well and his aim is accurate the sword in buried to the hilt into the bull which drops dead immediately as if an electrical switch was tripped. If the matador is at all sloppy, he keeps repeating his efforts until the bull dies. Such a fight is rather bloody and the crowd will have less respect for the matador who has also probably moved his feet too much. The bull is dragged from the arena by horses and delivered to a butcher who charitably disburses the beef to the poor.

The bullfight has its roots in ancient Rome but was refined in Spain to its present form. I have witnessed other so-called bullfights at *feria* (fair days) in smaller towns which had little resemblance to a real bullfight. One was in a town outside Madrid called Chinchón. Chinchón is the home of a common popular anise-based liquor of the same name. The liquor is popular throughout Spain.

What I witnessed in Chinchón was also a spectacle but one lacking in any civility or grace at all. Even if you regard bullfighting as cruel, which I must admit it is, in its pure form it can be graceful and inspiring. An old ruined bull was released into an arena where the public was invited to give it some passes without any cape work. A number of highly inebriated Spanish citizens, some of whom became seriously injured during the event, simply harassed the beast to violence. The bull was spared to presumably fight at the next year's *feria*.

As mentioned above, young bulls are never purposely shown a cape before a bullfight. Most often they are raised in an area of southern Spain known as Las Miasmas. It is a swampy place where the bulls must constantly slog through thick mud so as to develop their leg muscles and overall strength. These bulls are not the diminutive types of Mexican corridas. They are huge. However, cows are routinely tested for aggression just to assess their worth as breeding stock.

Once while visiting a ranch owned by a Spanish Air Force officer, I got into the arena with a cow. I thought that cows being cows they would be rather docile. They were not at all docile. I quickly realized she wanted to kill me. The arena had wood barricades behind which people like me could hide for protection. I got behind a barricade only to have the cow stick her horn through wood wall of the barricade in an effort to gore me.

About halfway through my tour in Madrid, a Chinese Red Army general joined the attaché group. He came to Madrid following a tour in Washington, D.C. He sought me out and persistently asked me questions about the Spanish armed forces. Apparently, China was following Spain's entry into NATO quite closely.

I then remembered an ethnic Chinese whom I had met when I was working in the Pentagon. He had been a U.S. Army colonel during the Korean War. According to him, he had administrated Chinese prisoners of war. He said he was then semi-retired and a beltway consultant on things to do with foreign military sales. He would invite me to three-martini luncheons from time to time and ask me questions about Spain. I would tell him certain things that were not classified or even official information. He could have obtained the same information through various open media sources. I now came to suspect he had been working for the Chinese government and that he had biographed and coded me as someone who would at least talk to Chinese people. I further suspected that was how the Chinese general seemed to know a lot about me.

The general invited my wife and me to receptions at the Chinese embassy in Madrid and on various attaché trips he tended to stay close to me. He always knew where the best Chinese restaurant was no matter where we were. The restaurant owners all seemed to know him well and would roll out the red carpet for him and his guests. I would answer questions from him but any information I gave him was benign and available via open source media. In turn, in a tit-for-tat way, I asked him a lot of questions and I developed quite a biography on him. He had served as a junior officer in the Red Chinese Army during the Korean War. I was curious about his intelligence network within Spain. I found it was largely based on Chinese restaurants. That surprised me but it was kind of logical in that it was readily and quickly ethnically exploitable for him.

* * * *

Toward the end of my tour the King approached me during a social event and said he understood I would be leaving Spain soon. I confirmed same. He invited me to join him and the Queen and their two princess daughters, Infanta Elena and Cristina, aboard the royal yacht for a review of the NATO fleet near Barcelona and as well the bestowal of the combat banner to the new Spanish navy aircraft carrier, the *Princípe de Asturias*. Queen Sofia was the godmother of that ship. I was very much honored in that I was the only attaché to be invited aboard the royal yacht. We reviewed 30 naval vessels representing nine NATO navies.

We were just friends enjoying a pleasant, sunny afternoon at sea together. The yacht was luxurious and it had a bar which was open. Life was good. My friend was the King of Spain but I felt like the King of Kentucky. Had I thought to say that, I think he would have said, "Yes, you are, Your Majesty." He was that kind of guy.

I left Spain with the distinction of having been the most prolific intelligence reporter of any military attaché in our embassy. The Defense Intelligence Agency recognized me with a special Defense Superior Achievement Medal. The Commander of the Sixth Fleet sent me a special letter commending my handling of the numerous ship visits by the Sixth Fleet to Spanish ports. The other attachés at the U.S. Embassy and my other co-workers gave me a nice send-off party. I was relieved of my duties and I went home.

One of the things I cherish about my time in Spain was getting into the unique bar culture there. For a short few days, I was in a Madrid hospital for a condition that proved non-life threatening. My window had a good view of a bar located across the street from the hospital where I could observe the comings and goings of the bar patrons. So, I studied them. One middle-aged male patron would invariably show up at his bar early in the morning for breakfast which consisted of a pastry or perhaps a piece of egg and potato-based *tortilla española* and a shot of brandy. Later in the morning, about ten o'clock or so, probably on a work break, he would return and have a beer or perhaps a *chato* (a small glass of wine) with some sort of *tapas* or finger-food. His bartender tended to function as his social secretary passing along messages from associates. If you needed to contact him, I gathered that's how you contacted him. Later in the day around the siesta hour, he returned to the bar for lunch and more dialogue with the bartender. The subject of my study tended to drink a good bit over the course of his day but always with food and never to excess. The Spanish people tend to be moderate people in terms of their daily habits but they do tend to imbibe quite a bit.

Then in the evening hours after work, he would return yet again to his bar often in company with members of his family where they would enjoy a late evening meal. The bar was the social center of his daily and family life. If you meet a Spaniard, and he wishes to entertain you, he will likely invite you to his bar instead of his home. His bar is where he really lives.

There's another level to bar life in Spain. The kind of bar you choose is a reflection of many things including your politics, interests and your affiliations. For example, there are *tapas* bars which are centered on the type of finger food they serve more than anything else. People who frequent them tend to have a string of such bars that serve their evening meal needs. They are much like convivial English pubs where people enjoy meeting other people. There are chess bars. Patrons of chess bars tend to go there to play chess. There are bullfighting bars. Patrons there are expected to discuss bullfighting. Some bars cater to bus drivers or taxi cab drivers whose professional interests coincide. Other bars tend to be politically focused as in communist or anarchist persuasions.

As an attaché, I would send lists of black-listed bars in specific ports to which U.S. Navy ships were scheduled to visit. For instance, I would warn our ships about visiting anarchist bars. Anarchists tend not to get along well with U.S. Navy sailors.

Of course, the bar life I describe might be significantly different today. I am remembering a time in the late eighties.

CHAPTER 12

Transition to Civilian Life

Before leaving Spain in 1989, I contacted via telephone the Bureau of Navy Personnel. Out of curiosity, I wondered what might be offered to me in terms of a subsequent assignment. I did not like the answer I was given. They were true to their word about me not expecting much warmth even though I had been well recognized by the Defense Intelligence Agency during my tour in Spain. I had also received stellar fitness reports or evaluations during my tour. I figured a big black spot had been placed on my record as a result of what I had done to get my last job.

The detailer told me of two options. First option was a shore assignment in the basement of the Bureau of Personnel managing forms. That was literally the ultimate in bureaucratic paper pushing. I gagged. I regarded it as an insult. The second option was that of Executive Officer on a tender or repair ship. At that time the Navy was assigning the first females to go to sea exclusively on tenders. I had nothing against female sailors going to sea but I did not want to be the point man in the effort. I knew it would involve dealing with the press that was focusing on the initiative including their pregnancy rates. Furthermore, tenders do not do fun things at sea. They largely stay in port and repair other ships. Also, tenders typically have a large legal holding company of troublesome sailors awaiting court-martial. They were generally dumped on the tender from other ships not able or willing to host court-martials. That would be a big hassle for the Executive Officer and not in keeping with what I had been doing in my career to date.

I informed my detailer of my intention to submit my resignation. I had more than 21 years of active duty service and was therefore eligible for retirement. I was 43 years old which meant I was young enough to pursue a new civilian career. I briefly considered asking to be designated as an intelligence officer. That would have opened up new avenues of potential advancement but I decided not to do so. I decided to leave the Navy.

I flew from Spain to Washington, D.C., where I was administratively processed out of the Navy at the Anacostia Naval Facility. I had quite a bit of unused leave so I was placed on terminal leave for about sixty days. I then flew to Connecticut where my wife is from. There I joined my wife and my family living with my in-laws for a period until we bought a house in Thomaston, Connecticut.

I thought I could parlay my language skills and my foreign military sales experience into a job with one of the larger defense contractors in Connecticut such as Sikorsky, Kaman, Pratt & Whitney or United Technologies Corporation. Unfortunately for me, my timing was terrible. The Berlin Wall was then falling and the Soviet Union was breaking up. The foreign military sales industry dried up quickly thereafter. I sent out about 600 resumes. I got two weak nibbles. I decided to change the focus of my job search. Naval officers inspect all the time. So, I decided to look at inspecting for a living. I already had a strong basic background in electromechanical systems and structural things.

At about the same time, the family lakeside cottage on Bantam Lake in Connecticut was utterly destroyed by a tornado. I devoted my efforts to rebuilding and replacing the structure with a four-bedroom log cabin style home. I helped family members build it and filled in some gaps in my knowledge about home construction.

Then I found a home inspection company which hired mostly retired military folks such as I. The company was owned by a retired Army officer operating out of Maryland. At that time, the company had something like 22 West Point graduates on the staff. They hired me, trained me and turned me loose in Connecticut. In fairly short order, I had six home inspectors working for me. We covered all of Connecticut and some of Massachusetts as well as New York State. I became President of the Southern New England Chapter of the American Society of Home Inspectors.

I was making decent money but when I paid off the mortgage on my home in Canton, CT, I decided to retire once again. My timing was perfect. I retired just before the real estate industry took a nose dive in 2008. Afterwards, my team of six home inspectors went down to only two inspectors.

In February 2014, I suffered a freak accident that came close to killing me. I was ice fishing for several days with some friends and their younger sons. We were staying at the family cottage on Bantam Lake. We were snowed- and iced-in, and could not extract our vehicles even after I scattered all the kitty litter I could find on the iced driveway in order to create the necessary traction for the wheels. We prevailed upon a mutual friend to help us. He sent his son to us with a better truck to pull us out. That truck proved to be inadequate as well. It was not getting the traction it needed so I decided to jump into the bed of the truck to add more weight to it. The driver gunned the truck back and forth until I was bucked off and went under the truck.

The truck ran over my body at least once. I experienced a good number of snap-crackle-pop sensations which left me trying to guess which of my bones were breaking. Many of my ribs broke under the force of being run over. At least one broken rib punctured my right lung. I rather quickly began to spew blood out of my mouth onto the snow upon which I was laying. That dismayed me and I tried to put a good face on my situation in front of my friends by standing up and beating upon my chest to show them I was still functional. The trouble was I had more grave injuries than I knew at that moment. I could not get up. I had a broken pelvis as well as one or two crushed vertebrae and a broken shoulder blade plus a broken collar bone. I was an inch or so away from having a truck tire pass over my neck and spine and breaking both.

My friends summoned an emergency medical team from a local hospital. They put me on a stretcher and then man-handled me up the steep driveway to an ambulance. Fortunately, the temperature in the ambulance was set to tropical. I was very cold having been resting on the snow and ice for far too long. They cut my coat off and put a needle in my arm, and we went to a hospital that was about a half hour drive away. I woke up in the hospital. Things quickly got worse after they gave me some sort of cocktail of drugs that put me under into a deep narcoleptic trance for some long time. I had the worst dreams of my life. Many of the dreams had to do with imagined or real situations in Vietnam. While I was unconscious, my punctured long caused my chest cavity to fill with fluids thereby causing both of my lungs to collapse. I was placed on an oxygen feed but I wasn't keeping up. So, they went in through my back to conduct lung surgery and re-inflate my lungs. That was successful but it caused a blood clot or thrombosis to form in my right arm which blew up like Popeye's arm. I was very lucky the clot did not end up in my brain or other valuable body parts.

The surgery left me with a long ugly scar on my back. Later, I considered hiding that scar with a tattoo of a truck tire tread but I decided very few people would see my back anyway. My wife and my two daughters were wonderful aides and nurses to me. They did their best to prevent me from constantly pulling out the numerous tubes connected to my body.

When I gained some degree of lucidity, I began to question my wonderful caregivers about what medications they were giving me. I discovered they were giving me a lot of opioids for pain. I demanded they cease medicating me. I feared addiction. They were also giving me some powerful anti-anxiety medications. I told them I had no anxiety. Another great nurse practitioner told me I was well within my rights to refuse medications except for the blood thinners they gave me following the thrombosis that developed in my right arm.

I spent three and a half months in two hospitals and a rehabilitation center. During my stay, many friends and well-wishers visited me including dear friends from my days in Argentina.

Since then, I have recovered fairly well and I enjoy a pretty good life but I yearn for the adventure of my time in the Navy. When I dream at night I'm almost always back in the Navy. When I wake up, I'm in a much more mundane world.

A KENTUCKY BOY GOES TO SEA AS A NAVAL OFFICER

About the Author

U pon retirement from the Navy in 1989, Marshall V.S. Hall embarked on a new career as a home inspector. He joined a home inspection company staffed by mostly retired military officers. He has since fully retired and settled in the Albany, New York area.

www. hellgatepress.com

Made in United States
North Haven, CT
01 August 2022

22130947R00095